Participant Recruitment and Retention in Intervention and Evaluation Research

POCKET GUIDES TO
SOCIAL WORK RESEARCH METHODS

Series Editor
Tony Tripodi, DSW
Professor Emeritus, Ohio State University

AUDREY L. BEGUN
LISA K. BERGER
LAURA L. OTTO-SALAJ

Participant Recruitment and Retention in Intervention and Evaluation Research

OXFORD
UNIVERSITY PRESS

OXFORD
UNIVERSITY PRESS

Oxford University Press is a department of the University of Oxford. It furthers
the University's objective of excellence in research, scholarship, and education
by publishing worldwide. Oxford is a registered trade mark of Oxford University
Press in the UK and certain other countries.

Published in the United States of America by Oxford University Press
198 Madison Avenue, New York, NY 10016, United States of America.

CIP data is on file at the Library of Congress
ISBN 978-0-19-024503-0

1 3 5 7 9 8 6 4 2

Printed by WebCom, Inc., Canada

The work reflected in this book is dedicated to the many colleagues, mentors, and students with whom we have had the privilege of working over the years: they are too many to identify individually. Even more important to each of us, the work is dedicated to the many individuals who shared their time, energy, and experiences with us, as participants in the various studies discussed here, none of which could have been implemented without their generous engagement.

Contents

Preface

Empirically informed practice is a significant goal in many professions, including social work. As a result, professionals in social work and other fields depend on empirical studies that can be trusted as being methodologically sound and conducted with scientific integrity. Achieving this broad goal of scientific integrity requires investigators to develop and apply scientifically responsible research strategies at each phase of the research endeavor. One area with a powerful effect on a study's overall integrity concerns the soundness of the study sample: the quality of intervention research is dependent on the participation of adequate and representative samples.

Recognizing a gap in easily accessed research educational materials (see chapter 1), we decided to share lessons that we have learned about participant recruitment and retention through a review of the wildly scattered literature and sharing our own trial-and-error experiences (as well as our successes along the way). We designed this Pocket Guide for the benefit of the following audiences:

- investigators new to conducting intervention research, including students learning to engage in primary data collection for intervention studies,

- experienced investigators who are beginning to turn their attention to conducting intervention research, and
- practitioners in social work and other professions engaged in program evaluation efforts.

We designed the contents to be relevant for social work investigators and a transdisciplinary network of investigators from an array of disciplines such as medicine, nursing, education, psychology, counseling, criminal justice, occupational therapy, physical therapy, and other behavioral health, social science, and humanities disciplines where interventions with people are being empirically tested.

Following chapter 1, we introduce important concepts and place the problems of participant recruitment and retention in context. First, we present two distinct chapters: one each about participant recruitment (chapter 2) and participant retention (chapter 3). In our final two chapters we present content and tools useful to investigators in planning for the costs and resources necessary for successful participant recruitment and retention (chapter 4), as well as data analytic strategies and reporting formats related to study recruitment and retention (chapter 5).

Throughout the book, we discuss issues related to intervention and evaluation research ethics and the institutional review of research procedures involving human participants. We also present numerous concrete examples throughout the book—some represent successes and others more "crash and burn" experiences. Many examples come from our shared years of experience as center scientists with CABHR, the Center for Applied Behavioral Health Research (originally named the Center for Addiction and Behavioral Health Research) at the University of Wisconsin–Milwaukee's Helen Bader School of Social Welfare. Examples also are derived from one or another author's experiences prior to joining CABHR or since moving to the Ohio State University College of Social Work.

Participant Recruitment and Retention in Intervention and Evaluation Research

1

Introduction
and Context

The success of any intervention or evaluation study is dependent on the ability of investigators to recruit and retain appropriately representative and sufficient numbers of research participants (Berger, Begun, & Otto-Salaj, 2009; Hinshaw et al., 2004). However, investigators often overestimate their ability to engage and retain the types and numbers of participants needed to satisfy the demands of their study designs. Many research textbooks present elaborate and elegant descriptions of sampling plans for quantitative studies. The topics they address may include power analysis, sampling with and without replacement, snowball sampling, and other important lessons (for example, Alston & Bowles, 2013; Corcoran & Secret, 2013; Creswell & Plano Clark, 2011; Engel & Schutt, 2017; Faulkner & Faulkner, 2014; Grinnell & Unrau, 2014; Royse, 2011; Rubin & Babbie, 2016; Russell, 2014; Trochim, Donnelly, & Arora, 2016). The bibliography comparing textbooks about social work research methods compiled by Rubin (2009) includes sections devoted to important topics such as measurement, design, and evaluation; the topic of "sampling" is embedded in a section about survey research. Most of these resources present little or nothing concerning methods of participant recruitment and retention necessary for achieving study goals.

Two notable and refreshing exceptions to this trend are: (1) the Rubin and Babbie (2014) text, which includes six pages within a chapter about culturally competent research describing practices related to recruiting and retaining study participants, and (2) the text by Krysik and Finn (2013) which includes a nine-page summary of strategies for recruiting research participants.

Since most research training resources do not provide guidance specifically about effective participant recruitment and retention practices, novice researchers may be ill-prepared to succeed in participant recruitment and retention. Or, they may risk significant, expensive, time- and resource-intensive trial-and-error learning along the way. The literature to help inform participant recruitment and retention activities is scattered, fragmented across disciplines, and difficult to assemble.

Furthermore, individuals developing intervention research proposals often find it difficult to develop accurate estimates of the personnel and dollar costs that will be required for recruitment and retention activities. Available literature sources generally do not help investigators assess the cost-effectiveness or cost-utility of different approaches for recruiting intervention study participants. Overall, it appears that investigators' knowledge concerning intervention study participant recruitment and retention "is in its infancy" (Brown, Long, Gould, Weitz, & Milliken, 2000, p. 625).

As a result, underprepared intervention researchers may fail to recruit and retain sufficient and representative samples (Clay, Ellis, Amodeo, Fassler, & Griffin, 2003). Among a cohort of 41 intervention studies conducted in the early 1980s, fully one-third failed to successfully recruit even 75% of their target number of participants (Charlson & Horowitz, 1984). Two decades later, Thomson CenterWatch (2006) reported that more than 81% of clinical trials for medical interventions were delayed due to inadequate recruitment of participants. Kitterman, Cheng, Dilts, and Orwoll (2011) calculated the costs for a single research institution launching 260 studies that underenrolled participants (24% of all clinical studies conducted there): almost $1 million in a single year!

Analogous data concerning behavioral science and social work intervention research do not seem to exist; we have no good indication of how many or what proportion of social work or other behavioral health intervention studies fail for reasons related to inadequate recruitment or retention of study participants, or that end up being severely underpowered (more on this topic later). Given the limited training and guidance provided to investigators concerning how to recruit and retain participants in intervention studies, the figures may be considerable.

This issue is particularly relevant to social work investigators, in part because social work scholars are recognized for engaging in studies that involve some of the most difficult populations to recruit and retain over time (Begun & Gregoire, 2014). This list includes:

- children and adolescents vulnerable to abuse or exploitation;
- individuals with cognitive impairments due to age, disease, mental disorder, developmental disability, or chronic substance abuse;
- individuals and families living without secure housing;
- men and women engaged with the criminal justice system;
- individuals and families with immigrant, refugee, or undocumented status; and,
- others.

Thus, it is crucial for social work investigators, as well as investigators from other disciplines and behavioral sciences, to employ efficient and effective techniques in both recruiting and retaining participants for their intervention and evaluation studies. The purpose of this book is to provide investigators in social work and other disciplines with knowledge and resources relevant to successfully planning, budgeting, and implementing participant recruitment and retention strategies when conducting intervention or evaluation research.

This introductory chapter addresses how participant recruitment and retention plans relate to a study's design demands and then how an intervention or evaluation study's overall integrity is affected by the soundness of the study sample. In addition, we define several key terms that apply to issues in participant recruitment and retention, terms that appear throughout the remaining book chapters.

RECRUITMENT AND RETENTION BY DESIGN

In conducting intervention research we may be attempting to learn whether a specific intervention has the desired effect and whether or not there were unintended, unexpected positive or negative side effects. Such efficacy studies typically involve relatively small numbers of participants—which seems to bode well for ease of meeting participant recruitment and retention goals. However, *efficacy studies also tend to involve interventions delivered under carefully controlled conditions to a highly homogeneous group of participants. Participant exclusion criteria, designed to reduce potential study confounds arising from participant variability, may be so restrictive that relatively few potential participants are eligible for inclusion. The example developed in Figure 1.1 demonstrates how a study's exclusion criteria applied to an initially large pool of individuals can easily result in too few participants eligible for inclusion in a planned study.

Effectiveness studies represent the next phase of knowledge building in a translational research cycle (see Begun & Gregoire, 2014).

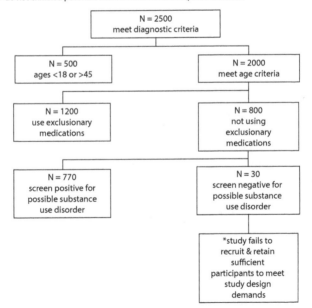

Figure 1.1 Impact of Exclusion Criteria: Hypothetical Intervention Study

Investigators address how well an intervention with demonstrated efficacy actually holds up under less controlled, more real-world conditions. Recruitment and retention in *effectiveness studies* involve larger numbers of participants, and include participants representing more heterogeneous, diverse populations. For example, whereas an efficacy study might include only individuals who have a single specific diagnosis, the next-phase effectiveness study may require recruitment and retention of individuals presenting with more complex clinical pictures and co-occurring problems. Or, participants representing different racial or ethnic groups, ages, genders, or geographical regions may appear in the planned study design (see Figure 1.2). Thus, investigators may need to engage in forms of stratified, targeted recruitment in order to enroll and retain the requisite numbers and types of study participants to successfully answer the effectiveness questions.

Successful study recruitment and retention often requires a delicate balance between being both inclusive and exclusive in establishing and applying criteria for participant eligibility. On the inclusive side, an investigator may wrestle with the aim of reaching a wide range of potential participants to include; for example, members from rare or underrepresented segments of nonhomogeneous populations (Castro, Harmon, Coe, & Tafoya-Barraza, 1994). On the side of being more exclusive, investigators risk high participant dropout or low retention rates if they recruit individuals who end up unable to meet the demands of study participation (Brekke, 2005).

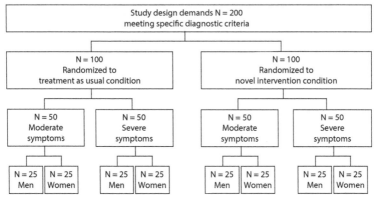

Figure 1.2 Stratified Sampling Plan: Hypothetical Intervention Study

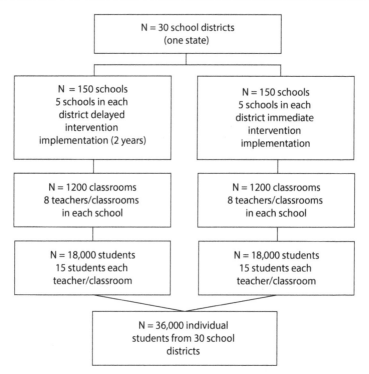

Figure 1.3 Hierarchical "Nested" Design: Hypothetical Intervention Implementation Study

Subsequently, in the translational science framework, implementation science examines how effective interventions are (or are not) adopted into general practice, and what factors might affect their adoption (or later de-adoption). Implementation study designs may require participant recruitment and retention in complex, multilevel, hierarchical sampling frameworks. For example, an implementation study might involve individual students "nested" within classrooms that are "nested" within schools, "nested" within school districts (see Figure 1.3).

As you can see, the nature of the participant recruitment and retention challenges vary by the nature of the intervention study at hand.

Retention in Longitudinal Research

With intervention research, we typically are interested in measuring change in conditions or outcomes targeted in our intervention efforts.

Because we are interested in evaluating change, intervention research studies frequently rely on longitudinal rather than cross-sectional research designs. One significant recruitment and retention challenge with longitudinal study designs is the necessity for maintaining participants' involvement over time. Should we wish to answer questions about the durability of our intervention's effects, we may need to engage participants through long-term, postintervention follow-up time frames, as well.

RECRUITMENT AND RETENTION: DESIGNING INTERVENTION RESEARCH WITH INTEGRITY

Systematic approaches to participant recruitment are needed in order to ensure a sound sample in quantitative studies. Three closely related topics are important to consider with regard to the general implications of adequate study recruitment and retention for intervention and evaluation studies: sample size, heterogeneity, and statistical power.

Sample Size

Simply stated, failure to attain an appropriate sample size—either through underrecruitment or insufficient retention—jeopardizes a study's validity and integrity. The matter of recruiting an adequate sample size is partly driven by basic assumptions involving the relationship between a sample and a population. As a reminder, inferential statistical analyses (such as an independent-groups *t*-test, paired *t*-test, or analysis of variance) allow us to test hypotheses and estimate population parameters based on samples properly drawn from populations. We design sampling approaches to minimize sampling error, thereby enhancing the extent to which our sample data accurately represent what we would see if we were actually able to measure the population as a whole. Statistical inference concerns results obtained from a sample being generalized to a population and relates to the study's external validity (Dattalo, 2008).

Quantitative study results and conclusions based on small sample sizes, compared to large sample sizes, are potentially more susceptible to bias introduced by sampling error (discussion of how to determine study sample size appears in chapter 4). A demonstration of this point

Table 1.1 How Sample Size Affects Population Representativeness: Green M&M's Example

Individual Students' M&M's counts				Aggregated Teams' M&M's counts			Aggregated Class M&M's counts		
# green	not green	total #	% green	# green	total #	% green	# green	total #	% green
3	31	34	8.8%						
5	32	37	13.5%	19	115	16.5%			
11	33	44	25%						
4	34	38	10.5%						
5	26	31	16.1%	13	107	12.1%			
4	34	38	10.5%				67	447	15%
3	36	39	7.7%						
4	34	38	10.5%	13	119	10.9%			
6	36	42	14.3%						
11	37	48	22.9%						
9	18	27	33.3%	22	106	20.8%			
2	29	31	6.5%						
Reported green M&M's population[a]								16%	

[a] This estimate is per https://www.exeter.edu/documents/mandm.pdf, which also states that the Mars Candy Company no longer publishes the proportions of colors in the M&M's product line.

is presented in Table 1.1, based on data collected with an undergraduate research class (this active learning exercise was suggested by Marchant-Shapiro, 2013). The population parameter estimates for the proportion of green M&M's candies based on each individual student's sample were far more variable (6.5%–33.3%) and less accurate than what was achieved by combining their smaller, independent samples into a single larger sample (15%). The take-home lesson: the larger sample sizes more closely approximate the true population of 16% green M&M's produced (although there remained some sampling error, students insisted they did not eat any before the exercise was complete).

Sample Heterogeneity

Ensuring generalizability of a sample to the population from which it was drawn also requires sufficient diversity within the sample to reflect the population's diversity. Thus, sampling efforts need to be sufficiently inclusive if study results are going to adequately reflect the population's natural heterogeneity. Investigators might want to become more informed about strategies for promoting culturally competent research and the development of culturally competent interventions (e.g., Delva, Allen-Meares, & Momper, 2010; Farmer & Farmer, 2014; Harvard Catalyst, 2010; Lee & Zaharlick, 2013; Tran, Nguyen, & Chan, 2017). Grinnell and Unrau (2014) cautioned investigators to attend to a study's cultural acceptability and carefully consider the cultural sensitivity of the research questions, measures, and all study procedures; through an extension of logic, we can apply this advice to recruitment and retention strategies, as well.

Wang, Aminawung, Wildeman, Ross, and Krumholz (2014) presented a cogent example demonstrating the importance of attention to sample representativeness. The team examined 14 longitudinal studies which, when combined, involved over 72,000 participants. The authors analyzed patterns by which participants were at risk of being lost to follow-up as a function of incarceration, given the disproportionately high rates of black men incarcerated in the United States. The risk of longitudinal study attrition among black men due to incarceration was estimated to range as high as 65% across these studies (depending on study duration). Two profound implications of these findings for intervention research integrity include the loss of statistical power and the strong risk of underestimating disparities that exist for black men compared to other groups in a study.

Specific participant recruitment and retention issues, recommendations, and examples are presented in chapters 2 and 3. In this introduction, it is helpful to consider three general principles: heterogeneity, use of language, and size of the local "pool."

Heterogeneity Includes an Array of Relevant Features

We are used to thinking about some important demographic features, such as race or ethnicity; sex, gender, sexual or gender identity, and sexual orientation; socioeconomic status; national origin; geographical areas (local, state, regional, or national); religion, religiosity, and spirituality; and age, which might be as much about cohort as it is about developmental or chronological age. Superimposed over these features we might also need to consider recruiting and retaining participants heterogeneous across additional factors that are relevant for intervention studies: the participants' diagnostic categories, symptom severity, and presence/absence of co-occurring problems; ability and disability; cognitive functioning; living conditions; prior or current intervention, treatment, and self-change attempts; and, past or present experiences with discrimination, oppression, prejudice, and stigma. "Cultural" sensitivity expressed by investigators is "about being sensitive to the individuals, families, and communities," and "steps taken to be responsive to the needs of the study participants" (Delva, Allen-Meares, & Momper, 2010, p. 60). It is not specifically about a list of characteristics, per se.

Careful Use of Language Is Critically Important

Investigators' use of language is more than a consideration of the "tongue" or dialect used (e.g., English, Spanish, French, Italian, Korean, Hmong, Vietnamese, Navajo, Dakota, or Somali). With careful, intentional use of language we can avoid unintentional expressions of bias, prejudice, stigma, and stereotyping (see Begun, 2016; Broyles et al., 2014). Consider, for example, the difference between two studies: one recruiting "victims of domestic violence" and the other recruiting "adults who have experienced violence in an intimate partner relationship." Many individuals from whom we might like to hear consider themselves to be survivors, not victims; they are not likely to enroll in the first study. Furthermore, intimate partner or relationship violence terminology is more inclusive of varied relationship types (e.g., dating and ex-partner relationships) than terms like "marital" or "domestic violence." Recruitment using the more inclusive type of language is likely to engage a larger number and wider range of study participants. In short, the language that we use may make all the difference in terms of how potential participants might respond to study recruitment efforts.

The Local "Pool" from Which an Investigator Might Be Recruiting May Be "Shallow"

This is problematic because of the principle that medical researchers have dubbed Lasagna's Law[1]: the observation that investigators all too often commit the error of (grossly) overestimating the pool of potential study participants who meet a study's inclusion criteria and the number they can successfully recruit into the study (Thoma, Farrokhyar,

---

[1] Lasagna's Law was named after the clinical pharmacologist and drug development scientist, Louis Lasagna (see Thoma, Farrokhyar, McKnight, & Bhandari, 2010).

McKnight, & Bhandari, 2010). This phenomenon was named after the clinical pharmacologist who observed that clinical trial investigators often overestimate the number of appropriate patients who may be willing to participate in research studies (Gorringe, 1970). A survey of medical investigators found that Lasagna's Law frequently operated in primary care research (van der Wouden, Blankenstein, Huibers, van der Windt, Stalman, & Verhagen, 2007); we believe that Lasagna's Law is often reflected in social and behavioral intervention research, as well. In today's world, this effect may be amplified by faulty assumptions driven by social media; investigators may be misled by enthusiasm expressed by a vocal minority, erroneously concluding that the depth and breadth of interest in the researched topic is far greater than actually exists. While social media can reach large numbers of individuals, there is considerable bias introduced. The result is that passionate expressions in social media do not necessarily translate into sufficient interest to attract study participants (Yuan, Bare, Johnson, & Saberi, 2014).

The "shallow pool" problem is compounded when it becomes difficult to protect each participant's anonymity or confidentiality within small, tightly networked communities. Furthermore, in the "shallow pool" scenario, investigators run the risk of overstudying the same participants within a community. On one hand, multiple investigations of the same individuals experiencing the same rare condition or circumstances can result in what we might call population fatigue—they become sick and tired of volunteering. On the other hand, we may also create a group of supervolunteers—those whom Abadie (2010) terms "professional subjects" or "professional guinea pigs." These individuals help fulfill recruitment goals of various studies, but come to overrepresent the same small group of individuals across all studies in a research area.

We do not know, for example, how many studies of HIV prevention interventions were conducted with the very same participants in the heavily studied San Francisco, Chicago, or New York areas. Not only do we run the risk that prior and concurrent participation in other intervention studies can confound outcome results of our own intervention study, as a scientific field we lose the benefit of independence between different studies in the overall knowledge-building process. Consider the lessons learned in the biomedical field through the story of Henrietta Lacks's cancer cells (see Skloot, 2010). In addition to the significant ethical

concerns, translational science encountered a major setback when therapies developed to the specific cell lines cultured from Henrietta Lacks's
cancer failed repeatedly in the more heterogeneous, real-world of many
different patients' cancers. Scientists became very good at destroying
Lacks-line cancers, but their solutions did not cure others in practice.
This is a serious risk when our studies involve individuals from rare or
underrepresented segments of the population (Castro, Harmon, Coe, &
Tafoya-Barraza, 1994). Because of these issues, a research clinical trials
database registry (www.verifiedclinicaltrials.com) has been developed
that facilitates the cross-checking of participant names by study investigators, in order to reduce the likelihood that research participants will
be concurrently enrolled in multiple clinical trials.

Statistical Power

Sample size is directly related to *statistical power*. In general terms, statistical power for an inferential analysis reflects the chances that the
investigator will draw a correct inference from the data. The stronger
a test's statistical power, the better our chances for correctly rejecting a null hypothesis (the hypothesis of no difference between a treatment and control group, for example). In intervention research terms,
increased power means that we improved our ability to detect an existing intervention effect: we reduced our chances of inappropriately failing to reject the null hypothesis when we should have done so (Sink &
Mvududu, 2010). This is sometimes referred to as reducing the probability of a Type II error (see Figure 1.4). With underpowered studies, we
run the risk of not finding effects from our interventions when, in fact,
the intervention actually had an impact on outcome variables.

Weak statistical power arises from multiple sources, but small sample sizes are a contributing factor and result in a reduced probability of
detecting a true effect in the data (Rosenthal, 2012; Sink & Mvududu,
2010). Conducting scientifically responsible research requires enrolling
and retaining large enough numbers of participants to effectively test the
study's hypotheses (Berger et al., 2009; Hinshaw et al., 2004; Zweben et al.,
1994). Intervention researchers are encouraged to establish good estimates
of sample sizes necessary to achieve sufficient statistical power, in order
to ensure the scientific integrity, generalizability, and meaningfulness
of study results (Bell et al., 2008; Dattalo, 2008; Sink & Mvududu, 2010).

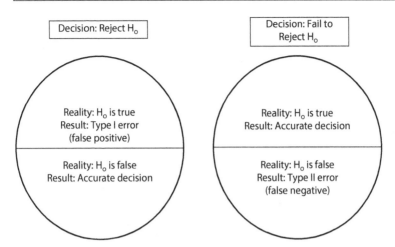

Figure 1.4 Type I and Type II Errors for Null Hypothesis (H_o) of No Intervention Effect

Scholars have challenged the ethical standing of intervention studies that suffer from external validity shortcomings on the grounds that the value of the knowledge gained does not warrant the risks to which participants have been exposed (Freedman, 1987; Halpern, Karlawish, & Berlin, 2002).

This discussion about sample size includes mention of effect size because a distinct relationship exists for which studies become reported in the literature. Slavin and Smith (2009) demonstrated the impact of a publication bias evidenced in their analysis of 185 educational intervention studies. They observed that large sample studies with small effect sizes are more likely to appear in the literature compared to small sample studies. In order for small sample studies to appear in the literature, their effect sizes have to be more impressive (Slavin & Smith, 2009). The actual computation of effect size is independent of sample size, a topic addressed in greater detail by Dattalo (2008); tools for calculating a study's necessary sample size are presented in chapter 4.

KEY TERMS AND CONCEPTS

So far, we have examined several important topics related to responsible and effective participant recruitment and retention in intervention and evaluation research. Several key terms and concepts arise in the remaining chapters that warrant explanation and exploration.

Intervention Versus Evaluation Research

In their introductory chapter, Fraser, Richman, Galinsky, and Day (2009) define intervention as an intentional change strategy comprising purposeful actions. Our interventions might be designed to resolve or reduce an identified problem or condition, to disrupt the pathway of risk or vulnerability factors that contribute to that problem or condition, or to enhance the resilience and protection factors related to that problem or condition. Thus, it is not all that difficult to distinguish between studies concerned with answering questions regarding the efficacy or effectiveness of interventions and those designed to answer other types of research questions or to test theory. A more subtle and difficult distinction exists between intervention research and evaluation research.

Turning once again to Fraser et al. (2009), intervention research can be differentiated from evaluation research in that the first involves the design and development of an intervention, whereas the latter assesses processes and outcomes related to existing interventions. The authors acknowledge that there exists considerable overlap in the methodologies used in both intervention and evaluation research. For the purposes of discussing participant recruitment and retention, it is likely that evaluation researchers will be recruiting from within a population of individuals currently engaged in a program or they will be studying the entire population of individuals served by the program under review. Intervention researchers, on the other hand, are more likely to be faced with the challenge of recruiting participants into the intervention and retaining them throughout the course of study, and addressing external validity/generalizability issues, as well.

Participants Versus Subjects

At this point, you may have noticed that we describe the individuals engaged in intervention studies as "participants" and seldom use the word "subjects" in writing about them. This is a philosophical matter, rooted in social work traditions and derived from changing ethical traditions in research involving human beings (e.g., see Corrigan & Tutton,

2006). In many areas of science, the objects of an investigator's attention were subjected to a variety of experimental conditions. Considering a person to be a research subject, or subject of research, can be dehumanizing in this "objectifying" way.

Grinnell and Unrau (2014) make a distinction between qualitative research as involving active participants and quantitative research as involving subjects lacking in individuality. However, we want investigators who engage participants in any of type of study to be constantly aware and respectful of the fact that these are real people, not objects of study (Begun, 2016). The word "participant" is important because it reminds us that these individuals have chosen to engage with us in these studies, be they quantitative or qualitative in nature; these individuals have elected to participate in the study, and we need to behave accordingly. Corrigan and Tutton (2006) provided a similar, interesting review of the historical shift in preference for use of the term "participant" over "subject" in clinical research, and the American Psychological Association Publication Manual addresses this preferred use of language, as well (APA, 2009).

Participant Recruitment

In essence, recruitment refers to the process involved in bringing participants into and initially engaging them to be involved in a research study. Chapter 2 is entirely devoted to the topic of participant recruitment.

Participant Retention

Retention, on the other hand, is the process of keeping participants engaged with the study through the planned conclusion of their involvement. As discussed in chapter 3, factors affecting retention often arise earlier, during the recruitment and early study phases, not just later on. The processes of recruitment and retention are intertwined.

Participant Dropout or Attrition

First, the literature seems to use the terms "dropout" and "attrition" interchangeably. Second, consider two ways in which retention in an intervention study might fail. On one hand, a participant may quit or drop out of the intervention that is being studied. On the other hand, a participant may quit or drop out of the data collection aspects of the intervention study. Often, these occur simultaneously: the person simply disappears, is lost to follow-up, or invokes the right to withdraw from the intervention study all together.

Sometimes a person may quit participating in the intervention but be willing to continue providing data on the research measures. This scenario is what intention-to-treat study designs are all about. Employing strong retention efforts is particularly important for intention-to-treat analyses. These analyses include all enrolled or randomized participants in outcome comparisons between or among intervention study groups, regardless of intervention completion (Fisher et al., 1990). Therefore, if intervention research retention rates are low, intention-to-treat analyses may result in poorly estimated intervention effects (Grady, Cummings, & Hulley, 2001). In addition, if retention rates are low, important subgroup analyses may become impossible to conduct, which limits the inferences that can be drawn from an intervention study's results (Grady et al., 2001).

Participant Inclusion Versus Exclusion Criteria

The net result of specifying a study's inclusion and exclusion criteria is that investigators have clearly defined the specific population from which participants may be recruited. These sampling criteria thereby define the population to which a study's results can validly be generalized. Establishing inclusion and exclusion criteria is an integral part of study design and planning. As an example of clarity in defining the inclusion criteria, consider the *Support Matters* intervention study engaging 30 dyads (pairs) of participants, individuals reentering the community following a period of incarceration and a key support person for each of them:

> Prisoners eligible for study participation included male reentering prisoners who screened positive for a history of substance-use disorders, were 18 years or older, planned to be released to the county of the urban study site, were fluent English speakers, and were cognitively able to understand the demands of study participation. Eligible support

partners were those who indicated they did not use illicit substances, did not drink to the point of intoxication on a weekly basis, did not have a history of violence with the prisoner, were not under criminal justice supervision within the past year, were 18 years or older, were fluent English speakers, and were cognitively able to understand the requirements of participation. (Pettus-Davis et al., 2015, p. 60)

Measurement issues, over and above those related to testing study hypotheses, might be involved with study inclusion/exclusion criterion points. As an example, consider a study of individuals' personal histories with engaging in formal, informal, and self-change attempts to reduce their alcohol use before and after entering into treatment for an alcohol use disorder (Begun, Berger, & Salm-Ward, 2011). It was important that participants in this study be cognitively able to provide reliable retrospective self-report data, especially since we know that long-term, heavy alcohol use can result in diminished cognitive capacity. One of the study's inclusion criteria involved being able to "pass" (meet criteria on) the Trail Making Test, Parts A and B (Bowie & Harvey, 2006; Reitan, 1959); this measurement task was separate from measurement of study variables designed to answer the study's research questions.

Two key points to keep in mind are (1) the need for a clear, solid, and explicable rationale for the study-specific inclusion and exclusion criteria, and (2) a solid measurement plan related to these criteria. The rationale might include factors such as convention in the area of research or practice, the threshold at which a phenomenon becomes relevant to the study aims, or enhancing the extent to which the group of participants will mirror future recipients of the tested intervention under real-world conditions or in real-world settings. The measurement tools for screening around study inclusion/exclusion criteria are likely to differ from those used in the study itself: the inclusion/exclusion information gathered does not become data, per se—especially since the initial study screening information may be gathered prior to consent.

Random Selection Versus Random Assignment

Another distinction that can be confusing to those just beginning to learn about research methodology arises from the use of the word "random" in describing two very different procedures. *Random selection* refers to the way investigators generate a study sample that is reflective and representative of the larger population to which the study results are going to be generalized (external validity). For example, if we were interested in learning about the impact of a new parenting education intervention delivered to mothers in prison, we would not attempt to recruit every one of the estimated 65,600 mothers in state and federal prisons (based on 2007 data; Glaze & Maruschak, 2008). Instead, we would hope to test our intervention with a subset of women representative of the whole population of incarcerated mothers interested in parenting education opportunities—not the whole population of mothers, nor even the whole population of incarcerated mothers. We might implement a set of random selection procedures to generate this representative subset (sample). These are the kinds of sampling strategies well described in many research textbooks, often in chapters about survey research.

Random assignment, often colloquially called *randomization,* has a different goal and is used at a different point in the intervention research process. Once we have begun to randomly select our participants, our study design might call for us to assign these recruited individuals to experience different intervention conditions. For example, in our hypothetical study described in the previous paragraph, we might assign half of the women to a "treatment as usual" (TAU) group and the other half of the women to the experimental condition, receiving the new parenting education intervention. In order to ensure that we do not have unbalanced groups (such as the TAU group being significantly older, or having younger children than the group receiving the new intervention), we apply procedures to randomly divide our total sample of women into the two groups. We might use a lottery system or apply random digit generator software to determine which women belong in each study group. This is no longer about generating a sample representative of the population (that earlier external validity, generalizability issue). It is now about ensuring initial equivalence between our study groups. This enhances the extent to which we can conclude that our study results reflect differences in the intervention conditions, rather than effects of confounding variables (an internal validity issue); these methods may not always work to achieve this equivalence, but should at least reduce the differences between groups. Clearly, both random sampling and random assignment (randomization) are important to scientific integrity, but it is important to understand the difference in their aims.

Research Ethics

While social work investigators are often well informed about professional and research ethics in general, they may not be sufficiently prepared to anticipate or address ethical dilemmas that arise in the process of planning or implementing an intervention study. Recruitment and retention of participants in intervention studies involves several fairly specific ethical concerns. Examples of ethical issues include:

- the need to plan for study termination, especially when the intervention has been working well for some participants;
- dilemmas surrounding control group and TAU study designs, especially "no treatment" as a control condition;
- participants being able to distinguish treatment activities from research activities; and,
- participants' incentive payment issues.

Worth exploring is the discussion by Solomon, Cavanaugh, and Draine (2009) concerning ethical considerations involved with randomization procedures arising in the conduct of randomized controlled trials.

CHAPTER SUMMARY

Through intense focus on issues, processes, and practices related to participant recruitment and retention, this book assists investigators in social work and other fields in planning and implementing intervention research studies that can generate sound and impactful scientific knowledge. Unique contributions of this book are: (1) distillation and consolidation of principles and ideas from many dispersed sources and disciplines; (2) an emphasis on intervention research challenges related to participant recruitment and retention; and, (3) planning maps and practical tools ready to employ and adapt for a reader's own studies. This introductory chapter provided readers with an overview concerning the significance of strong participant recruitment and retention to research validity, integrity, and ethics. The topics and key terms discussed in this introduction pave the road to subsequent chapters that delve more deeply and provide practical tools for successfully recruiting and retaining participants in behavioral intervention studies.

2

Participant Recruitment

Carefully planned, scientifically responsible, and ethically imple-mented approaches for recruiting participants are needed to ensure the generalizability (external validity) of the study's results. Cost-effective recruitment activities also are necessary for enrolling large enough numbers of appropriate participants to adequately test the study hypotheses (Hinshaw et al., 2004; Zweben et al., 1994). In intervention and evaluation research, participant recruitment is best characterized as a continuous process, beginning with initial outreach through the act of randomizing subjects into study conditions (Spilker & Cramer, 1992). Scientifically responsible and cost-effective recruitment strategies should be taken into consideration during all phases of the recruitment process in intervention research.

The purpose of this chapter is to assist investigators to realistically estimate the number of individuals who may be willing to participate in a particular research study, and to maximize participant yield of their recruitment efforts while upholding scientific integrity. The chapter[1] begins with an examination of several strategies that can be undertaken

---

[1] Portions of this chapter are reprinted, with permission, from Berger, Begun, and Otto-Salaj (2009).

as part of developing a recruitment plan. The second part of the chapter describes methods related to participant recruitment.

PLANNING FOR RECRUITMENT

The following planning strategies can help at the outset of developing an intervention or evaluation research study. These strategies, part of a larger approach of solid study preparatory background work, are as follows:

- obtaining accurate prevalence or incidence rates,
- planning for diversity,
- conducting sound pilot work,
- dedicating adequate study resources to participant recruitment and retention.

In this chapter, we explore the first three of these in detail; the last we examine in chapter 4.

Estimating Prevalence and Incidence Rates

The first strategy involves obtaining accurate prevalence or incidence rates, or other numeric indicators of the population experiencing the study phenomenon of interest. For example, in working with a research team to develop a study in which pregnant women who had consumed alcohol were to be recruited, the outpatient clinic's staff indicated that "enough" pregnant women screened positive for alcohol use: an estimated 30 per year. Yet, when actual program data were examined, the staff were surprised to learn that the rate was much lower than anticipated: only three per year. Perhaps the high degree of concern about alcohol-exposed pregnancy made these few incidents stand out in their minds and seem more common than they actually occurred.

This example points to the importance of obtaining the best possible, accurate prevalence and/or incidence rates in terms of the target phenomenon to be studied. *Prevalence* rates indicate the total number of existing cases or incidents of the phenomenon of interest at a specific point in time, divided by the size of the relevant population, resulting in a prevalence ratio. *Incidence* rates are usually expressed as a ratio of the number of new cases or incidents of the phenomenon of interest, during a specified time frame, divided by the relevant population. For example, the prevalence of mental disorder among individuals with Down syndrome in Glasgow (United Kingdom) was estimated to be 10.8%, whereas the 2-year incidence rate of mental disorder was estimated to be 3.7% of persons with Down syndrome (Mantry et al., 2008). The difference in these statistics reflects a difference between who has had the problem of interest over time and for whom it has recently developed. As another example, the prevalence of autism spectrum disorders in the United States was estimated to be 10–20 persons per 10,000 in the general population (or 1–2 per 1,000), whereas in 2002 the incidence was estimated to be 3,000 new cases per year (www.rightdiagnosis.com/a/autism/prevalence.htm). In other words, incidence provides information about the likelihood of having a condition; prevalence provides information about how pervasive the condition is in a population. The relevance of this distinction has to do with the nature of the intervention—is it aimed at existing cases or at preventing the emergence of or early detection of new cases? This, in turn, influences the size and depth of the potential recruitment pool for the planned intervention study.

A variety of methods can be used to obtain accurate prevalence or incidence rates. A few of the more common ones include the use of:

- globally, nationally, regionally, statewide, county-wide, or locally representative datasets;
- administrative databases maintained at agencies, programs, or other study sites; and,
- previously published research.

Social indicator data are often particularly useful, such as the United Nations data presented on their economic and social development website (http://unstats.un.org/unsd/demographic/products/socind/). Regarding nationally and/or locally representative datasets, the Association of College & Research Libraries (ACRL) maintains a "Social Work Liaison's Toolkit: Data Sets" resource in which data sets as related to social welfare issues are listed (ACRL, n.d.). Other examples include the Treatment Episode Data Set (TEDS) and the Drug Abuse Warning Network (DAWN), supported by the Substance Abuse and

Mental Health Services Administration (SAMHSA; http://wwwdasis. samhsa.gov/webt/information.htm and http://www.icpsr.umich.edu/ content/SAMHDA/index.html). Or, the Health Indicators Warehouse can be consulted, through which the Centers for Disease Control and Prevention (CDC) present data on a number of health-related conditions and behaviors (www.healthindicators.gov).

Locally available options might include state government agencies, university survey centers, and nonprofit planning councils. When partnering with local agencies or programs to conduct a study, these organizations often make data available in order to develop planning figures for those particular study sites. Previously published research in the topic area of interest may be a best available option, if the information is relatively recent. Triangulation strategies by which multiple approaches are integrated into a single estimate are also worth considering, especially when locale-specific data are not available, or when a study involves unique or hidden populations. An important note of caution is that reports often confuse prevalence and incidence, so they should be interpreted with care.

Together, these methods can be used to approximate prevalence or incidence rates, but cannot necessarily provide an accurate count of individuals' willingness to participate in a particular research study. It is helpful for investigators to think about participant recruitment as a process rather than simply as an outcome.

Planning for Diversity

As discussed in chapter 1, study integrity hinges on the representativeness of the study sample with respect to diversity in the population for whom the tested interventions were designed to serve. Policy efforts supporting the recruitment of representative samples include the National Institutes of Health (NIH) policy on the inclusion of women and minorities in clinical research (October 2001; see http:// grants.nih.gov/grants/guide/notice-files/NOT-OD-02-001.html). This policy is mandated by federal law (http://history.nih.gov/research/ downloads/PL103-43.pdf) and responsive to the ethical principle of justice as outlined in the Belmont Report (http://www.hhs.gov/ohrp/ humansubjects/guidance/belmont.html#xselect). The justice principle addresses fair and equitable distribution of the costs and benefits of research participation; this includes fairness in both access to and sharing the burden for engaging in potentially beneficial research.

Recruiting diverse, representative samples is complicated when willingness to participate in research differs between population groups (Clay, Ellis, Amodeo, Fassler, & Griffin, 2003; Shavers, Lynch, & Burmeister, 2002). For example, members of certain groups may be suspicious of the potential personal risks of the intervention research or the potential for exploitation because of past research abuses, as in the Tuskegee syphilis study (Brandt, 1978) or the story of Henrietta Lacks (Skloot, 2011). More recently, the case of the Havasupai Tribe in Arizona highlights the fact that willingness may be impeded by experiences of conflict and mistrust of researchers. Specifically, the tribe settled with the Arizona Board of Regents in 2010 to resolve a human participant conflict. Blood samples collected by a university researcher for the purpose of examining whether or not a particular genetic link to diabetes existed among tribe members, a disease greatly affecting their community, were later used to address additional research questions (Sterling, 2011). Members of the tribe had signed an informed consent containing broad language about the study purpose (Harmon, as cited in Sterling, 2011); yet, tribe members believed their blood samples would only be used for the diabetes study (*Havasupai Tribe v. Arizona Board of Regents*, as cited in Sterling, 2011).

The point is that the trust of potential research participants may have been violated by others in the past, which in turn may affect their willingness to participate in future studies. Willingness to participate may be influenced by an individual's or group's concerns about stereotyping, damage to the reputation of their racial or ethnic group, or policy implications of the research results (Sage, 1994). Still others may have past personal experiences of racism or discrimination associated with seeking or obtaining access to social work or behavioral interventions, or they may have concerns about stigma associated with receipt of the services being studied (McKay, 2005; Snowden, 2005). Finally, those who have participated in previous studies may base their willingness to participate now on their prior experiences with researchers.

Conducting Pilot Studies

The next strategy in our list involves conducting sound pilot studies. To put this issue into context, consider the four steps undertaken to develop new clinical interventions. According to the NIH (2012), Phase I involves testing a newly developed intervention among a small number of individuals to determine efficacy and assess safety; Phase II studies apply the intervention among a larger number of individuals to continue to determine efficacy and further assess safety; Phase III studies involve comparing the intervention to other interventions to determine efficacy and monitor safety in a larger number of individuals and collect information about safe use; and Phase IV studies examine the intervention after its release to the public in order to monitor effectiveness and collect widespread safety information. In work related to these phases, Czajkowski, Powell, and Spring (n.d.) propose questions related to recruitment as part of pilot work prior to conducting a Phase III study. Specifically these questions include estimating protocol acceptability among participants and protocol feasibility in terms of the number of participants screened who are actually enrolled into the study.

Protocol Acceptability and Feasibility

Investigators may conduct initial pilot studies to develop estimates of participant willingness to engage in a planned research study. Acceptability questions assess participants' comfort with various aspects of both the research protocol and the intervention protocol, including the various intervention components, as well as the research data collection procedures. In addition, it is important to consider the distinction between a protocol element being acceptable to a person and a person being comfortable with it—in behavioral research we often engage participants in uncomfortable discussions that are, at the same, acceptable to them as part of the clinical process (see Broyles, Rosenberger, Hanusa, Kraemer, & Gordon, 2012).

Examples of acceptability questions include "Was any aspect of this [intervention or] questionnaire distressing to you?" and "If so which [part(s) or] question(s)?" (Austin, Colton, Priest, Reilly, & Hadzi-Pavlovic, 2013). Another acceptability question comes from a study where we asked hospitalized medical patients to rate on a 5-point scale: "How comfortable would you be in speaking with an alcohol and other drug counselor in the community via a secure video call or webcam?" A common acceptability rating scale (e.g., Mahoney, 2009) is:

| not at all acceptable | slightly acceptable | moderately acceptable | very acceptable | completely acceptable |

Qualitative methods such as focus group, face-to-face, and phone-based interviews may also be used to assess participant acceptability and the overall feasibility of both the intervention and research protocols (e.g., Kingston et al., 2014).

RECRUITMENT METHODS

In this section we present a model for organizing various participant recruitment methods for intervention and evaluation research. The presented methods focus on both direct and indirect recruitment strategies. *Direct recruitment methods* are those that reach potential participants directly, such as advertisements and flyers. *Indirect recruitment methods* include an intermediary, such as treatment providers referring clients or patients to a study. There are distinct advantages and disadvantages associated with each type of strategy, and evidence suggests that different participant recruitment strategies elicit responses from individuals at different points in their personal readiness to change process and from individuals experiencing varied levels of the focal problem (Webb, Seigers, & Wood, 2009).

Ideally, recruitment methods are implemented from an intentional plan. Figure 2.1 depicts a four-step process.

The formal recruitment process might be visualized in terms of a funnel, beginning with the widest possible "casting of a net" to inform potential volunteers about a study, then applying a series of filters that systematically exclude individuals who are ineligible or disinterested (Clay et al., 2003; Spilker & Cramer, 1992). A well-developed study recruitment plan accounts for all necessary details, at each step, allowing investigators to capitalize on each potential participant's initial interest. For example, in one intervention study our team ran a series of television advertisements about alcohol treatment. Unfortunately, study personnel were not available to answer phones immediately after the ads ran, resulting in missed recruitment opportunities. A better-developed plan would have included ensuring that project staff were prepared to handle calls in anticipation of the advertisements being aired.

Here we explore each of the four steps that would have been helpful in developing and refining the study's recruitment plan: generating

Figure 2.1 Stepped Recruitment Process in Intervention and Evaluation Research

initial contacts (directly and indirectly), screening, consent, and enrollment.

Generating Initial Contacts: Direct Approaches

The goal of this first step is to engage in activities that help build connections between the pool of potential participants and the study: getting the word out. Initial contacts may be generated within a particular study site, agency, or program. Or, they may be generated across local, regional, or national communities. As most participant recruitment for intervention research occurs at the local or regional level, it is important to know your local community and to build community trust when generating initial participant contacts for intervention research. For example, in an intervention study addressing co-occurring substance use and HIV risk for women, we mailed flyers to specific postal zip code areas as an "oversampling" outreach effort to ensure representation by women in the African American community. The message contained in the flyer asked recipients if they knew a woman who needed help rather than asking if they themselves needed help (see Box 2.1), a strategy adopted to avoid women believing they were being unfairly targeted or suspected as having an alcohol or drug problem. This approach proved successful

---

Box 2.1 Sample Participant Flyer for Intervention Research

Do You Know a Woman Who Needs Help?

Do you know a woman who is at least 18 years old, concerned about her drinking and/or drug use, and is thinking about stopping? If so, she may qualify to participate in a national research study and receive individual, confidential counseling at no cost.

Call:

Heart to Heart
(phone number)

Helping Women Make Healthy Choices

in generating initial contacts from a diverse group of potential participants. In this study, it was also observed that an open and trusting study environment led study participants to serve as informal referral sources for other members of their community ("word of mouth" advertising).

Other methods of generating initial participant contacts with a wide reach include media strategies for television, radio, and major newspaper advertising, as well as advertisements used within mass-transit systems (see Figure 2.2).

Although generally effective, media strategies may need to be counterbalanced with other strategies in order to generate representative samples. In an analysis of recruitment tactics used in pharmaceutical company drug trials, most used only a small number of "traditional" strategies, such as physician referrals and newspaper or radio advertisements (Lamberti, Mathias, Myles, Howe, & Getz, 2012). This disadvantaged the studies, as enrollment increased as a function of using a greater number of, and more nontraditional, tactics.

Alcohol Problems?

If you are 21 years of age or older, concerned about your drinking and serious about stopping alcohol use, you may qualify to participate in a national research study. Qualified participants will receive investigational medication and/or individual therapy free of charge.

Call us for more information at:
Center for Addiction and Behavioral Health Research

Clinical Research Unit located at Sinai Samaritan Medical Center
(414)xxx-xxxx

Figure 2.2 Sample Newspaper Advertisement for Intervention Research

The significance of this counterbalanced effort is highlighted in research demonstrating risks to generalizability resulting from different recruitment strategies: for example, differences between media-solicited and population-based participants. In a study of individuals' natural recovery from alcohol dependence (i.e., without formal assistance), nonabstinent recovery was reported by 17.3% of media-solicited participants but 81.8% among a population-based sample (Rumpf, Bischof, Hapke, Meyer, & John, 2000). These two groups also differed along other important dimensions, such as triggers for natural recovery, severity of alcohol dependency, and life satisfaction (Rumpf et al., 2000). According to the study authors, the observed outcome differences, in part, may have resulted from differences in the recruitment rate of those who experienced less severe alcohol dependence to begin with, not perceiving themselves to have had a serious alcohol problem, and therefore being less likely to respond to media solicitation.

This same theme of diverse strategies to obtain representative samples has been discussed by Subbaraman and colleagues (2015). They found that employing multiple sources of recruitment yielded a more representative sample in an addiction recovery study. For example, social media sources generated a higher proportion of young people, whereas recruitment efforts through recovery organizations generated the most African American participants. Evidence suggests that African American individuals are less likely to respond to traditional recruitment approaches (Brown et al., 2000). Taken together, these reports highlight the need for varied methods in generating initial contacts as a means of ensuring a representative sample.

Generating Initial Contacts: Social Media

In recent years, social media tools have emerged as resources for participant recruitment; online platforms such as Facebook readily come to mind (Morgan, Jorm, & Mackinnon, 2013). Shao et al. (2015) analyzed recruitment costs and the participant diversity resulting from varied social media strategies with their global efficacy study of HIV/AIDS knowledge and HIV testing videos among English and Spanish speakers. They found the highest success rate (intervention survey completion, fastest recruitment yield, and low cost ratio) among English speakers with a tested marketplace-for-work system, Amazon Mechanical Turk (MTurk), and high success among Spanish speakers with Facebook. Similarly,

MTurk emerged as a cost- and time-effective mechanism in a feasibility study for a positive psychology intervention to increase well-being and social relationships, although the study authors pointed to high attrition rates and questionable sample generalizability as potential concerns (O'Connell, O'Shea, & Gallagher, 2014). Shere, Zhao, and Koren (2014) found that, compared to traditional methods (e.g., recruiting potential participants from healthcare settings via the assistance of providers), social media methods were more effective in increasing their recruitment rate of pregnant women into an intervention study (see Figure 2.3).

In their analysis of Facebook advertising, Resko et al. (2017) reported several important findings (see Figure 2.4). First, paid advertisements were viewed over 2.6 million times by over 240,000 unique individuals. Second, this strategy resulted in almost 5,000 visits to their survey website and 766 surveys were completed. Third, the cost per completed survey was $3.82. This use of social media advertising can be a cost-effective method for making initial direct contacts in study recruitment.

Social media recruitment methods also may include a number of noncommercial online platforms, such as study announcements placed on organizational websites and electronic message boards. Craigslist, a for-profit company with a relatively noncorporate culture (Craigslist About Factsheet, n.d.), is an option for placing advertisements to reach

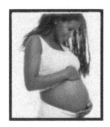

Currently Pregnant?

Help OSU researchers better understand how we might prevent early birth among Black women and receive a $50 Babies"R"Us gift card.

Figure 2.3 Sample Facebook Advertisement in Intervention Research

Source: Shared with permission via personal communication with Shannon Gillespie, College of Nursing, The Ohio State University, October 9, 2015.

If you are age 18-25 and living in Michigan please complete this short survey

Figure 2.4 Sample Facebook Advertisement, Michigan Young Adult Survey
Source: See Resko et al. (2017).

potential intervention research participants. To date though, it appears that venues like Craigslist and Facebook have been used more extensively to recruit participants into survey rather than intervention research.

Additional online technologies such as Twitter, tumblr, YouTube, and LinkedIn may help to spread the word about an intervention study. Twitter is a news or information sharing service (Perez, 2010), and tumblr is a social networking, microblogging website that especially attracts young users (Rifkin, 2013). LinkedIn, a social networking website, allows professionals to build networks of trusted colleagues (Rouse, 2015), and LinkedIn forum groups can be established to share information of professional interest, such as announcing a new study (Yuan et al., 2014). Much like Facebook and Craigslist, it appears at this time that these technologies are used more for recruitment into survey research. In a recent study of online social media and its effectiveness for recruiting HIV-positive participants to complete an online survey, Twitter and interactions on the study Facebook page were not significantly correlated with clicks on the investigators' Facebook ad (Yuan et al., 2014). These authors pointed out that the social media platforms helped to engage participants, and also engaged community professionals who serve the study population of interest. If such platforms are used in intervention research, dedicated staff time is required in order to tweet and network, generate "likes" of the project's Facebook page, monitor for disparaging posts, and maintain/refresh page content.

Institutional Review Boards (IRBs) may respond differently to varied social media approaches for generating initial contacts. For example, placing intervention research advertisements and announcements via social media in which communication is one-way appears to be more generally accepted (e.g., University of Pennsylvania IRB, 2015). Two-way communication in which an investigator sets up a social media account specifically for participant recruitment, such as a Facebook page, may not be recommended. Furthermore, the approaches may differ in effectiveness. For example, the Penn Medicine Office of Communications found that investigators had little recruitment success with two-way communication approaches due, in part, to the special accounts not being well-established "online destinations" for their target populations (University of Pennsylvania IRB, 2015).

Generating Initial Contacts: ClinicalTrials.gov
Another potential online source of spreading the word for intervention research is ClinicalTrials.gov, which is a searchable Web-based resource for the public to find information on publicly and privately funded clinical trials being conducted both at the national level and around the world (ClinicalTrials.gov, 2014). ClinicalTrials.gov is not a recruitment tool per se, but is a central location for the sharing of information about current, ongoing trials. ClinicalTrials.gov, maintained by the National Library of Medicine, was established as part of the Food and Drug Administration Modernization Act of 1997. By law, some studies must be listed in the registry, and with the Food and Drug Amendments Act of 2007 more studies are required to be registered, along with providing additional study information and study results (ClinicalTrials.gov, 2014). Sponsors and investigators may also voluntarily register studies (ClinicalTrials. gov, 2014). The strategy's recruitment power derives from the positive association between how responsive individuals are to recruitment messages and their self-identified need for intervention around a problem (Winslow et al., 2009).

Generating Initial Contacts: ResearchMatch.org
ResearchMatch.org is a secure, no-cost volunteer registry website. It was initially funded by the NIH, maintained by Vanderbilt University, and available to institutions granted a Clinical and Translational Science Award (CTSA). Since 2014, additional institutions meeting strict criteria have gained access to the website.

The ResearchMatch.org registry allows individuals to identify relevant studies that they might join, while allowing researchers with registry access to search profiles for potentially eligible volunteers (ResearchMatch, 2016). Researchers can then send a recruitment message to potential volunteers whose profiles are a good study fit. The messages are sent via ResearchMatch.org, as the researchers will not be provided with identifiable information until an individual responds "Yes" to learn more about the study. A Yes response will allow the researcher access to contact information without any obligation for an eligible individual to engage in the study (ResearchMatch, 2016). ResearchMatch.org differs from traditional ways of generating initial participant contacts as it allows individuals interested in potentially volunteering for a study to initiate contact with researchers versus the other way around. ResearchMatch.org is an example of using what may be an available institutional resource to help with participant recruitment.

Generating Initial Contacts: Agency Recruitment

As an alternative to wide-ranging, public direct methods, investigators might engage with established, formal referral systems among health and social services professionals and/or community agencies (Zweben, Barrett, Berger, & Murray, 2005). This might take many different forms, depending on the relationships that exist between entities. For example, a member of the investigative team might have a formal affiliation with the agency. In one of our studies, a member of the study team worked part-time for the children's hospital where recruitment was taking place for a study about establishing smoke-free homes for infants being discharged from the neonatal intensive care unit. By carefully identifying her researcher role, this facilitated engagement in IRB-approved recruitment activities within hospital units and outpatient clinics where she did not serve in her role as a hospital social worker.

Investigators and agencies might interact around participant recruitment by:

- agencies assisting with an outside investigator's study,
- investigators or evaluators assisting with or facilitating an agency's research, or
- a combination of these interactions.

Helpful suggestions and important caveats relate to each.

Agencies Assisting Outside Investigators

Investigators may engage with agencies around referring clients to an intervention study. Forming and maintaining effective partnerships with administrators of community-based agencies and establishing trusting and respectful relationships with potential referral sources is a tremendous advantage (Krysik & Finn, 2013; Leonard et al., 2003). Community-based participatory research principles (such as establishing collaborative, egalitarian roles between investigators and community members) serve to facilitate participant recruitment (and retention) in intervention studies, as well (Greiner et al., 2014; Israel, Schulz, Parker, & Becker, 1998).

These collaborative working relationships are not formed hastily: they evolve over many interactions, over long periods of time, and are dependent on the mutual partners' reputations with one another. Investigators need to avoid exploiting the agency, its staff, and its clients. For example, our team members have all presented in-service or continuing education trainings for community-based agencies, and at times have participated in an agency's staff meetings and fundraising events as part of the relationship-building process. Where positive, collaborative relationships exist, agencies may assist investigators in communicating with potential participants and making referrals to intervention studies (see Box 2.2).

Investigators/Evaluators Assisting Agencies

When outside investigators assist an agency with research or evaluation studies where their own clients will be engaged as participants, the line between practice and research should be starkly clear to both agency staff and the individuals being served. Individuals in these scenarios occupy two roles: client (or patient) and research participant. Thus, it is important to clearly distinguish for both staff and clients how the roles are distinct. At no point should a client be confused about services received as a client versus services received as a participant in an intervention study. In the client role, some degree of treatment effectiveness is to be expected, whereas when an intervention is being tested, it is understood that the intervention may or may not be effective (US Department of Health & Human Services, 1978).

In our own experience, one way to accomplish this distinction is to maintain separation between the roles of treatment provider and research intervention staff. Achieving this degree of separation can be facilitated by employing separate staff, and even separate offices

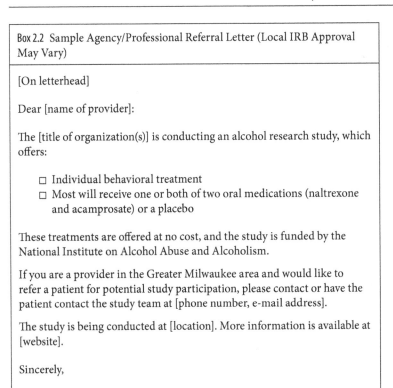

Box 2.2 Sample Agency/Professional Referral Letter (Local IRB Approval May Vary)

[On letterhead]

Dear [name of provider]:

The [title of organization(s)] is conducting an alcohol research study, which offers:

☐ Individual behavioral treatment
☐ Most will receive one or both of two oral medications (naltrexone and acamprosate) or a placebo

These treatments are offered at no cost, and the study is funded by the National Institute on Alcohol Abuse and Alcoholism.

If you are a provider in the Greater Milwaukee area and would like to refer a patient for potential study participation, please contact or have the patient contact the study team at [phone number, e-mail address].

The study is being conducted at [location]. More information is available at [website].

Sincerely,

[Name of Principal Investigator]

within an agency, as a means of minimizing a treatment provider's (unintended) undue influence over a client's decision to participate in research. This separation helps to uphold the research ethics principle of respect for persons by supporting autonomy in an individual's decision about study participation and upholds voluntariness in the informed consent process (US Department of Health and Human Services, 1978). For example, in evaluating an outpatient treatment program for women with substance use disorders, the project coordinator was not an agency employee and did not provide direct client services. Women were either self-referred or referred by treatment providers from the inpatient unit associated with the outpatient treatment program. The project coordinator was designated as the person to approach clients about participating in the evaluation study. She then conducted study-related baseline assessment and evaluation follow-up assessments with women who consented to participate in the study. Women who did not consent to participate continued to receive services from the agency with assurances that this decision would not alter the relationship with the agency.

In this evaluation study example, a woman received evidence-based treatment regardless of evaluation study participation. In the case where agency-based investigators would recruit their own clients for participation in a randomized controlled trial (RCT), the clients will receive either an intervention with unknown effectiveness or a control condition intervention (e.g., treatment as usual). As a result, the agency recruitment process would be modified. In this case, we would still recommend that research staff directly recruit clients, which delineates treatment provider and research intervention elements and roles. For example, consistent with the local IRB, a Health Insurance Portability and Accountability Act (HIPAA)-compliant service provider employed with the agency would first ask a client for his/her permission to have a research staff member speak with them about potential study participation. If the client provides permission and is interested in the study, the informed consent processes are then conducted by the research staff member. The major difference in this scenario compared to the evaluation scenario lies in the staff member's responsibility to ensure the client clearly understands the experimental nature of the intervention.

Finally, whether an agency is assisting an outside investigator in participant recruitment or an investigator/evaluator is assisting an agency, administrators and staff may feel pressured to enroll clients to satisfy grant goals or receive study dollars. Regular team meetings to promote collaboration, set realistic expectations from the beginning, develop ethical recruitment procedures, and team problem-solving help to successfully maximize recruitment efforts.

Screening

Once potential participants have been identified, the next step is to engage in screening to ensure that each is eligible to participate. Screening operationalizes the study's participant inclusion/exclusion criteria. As introduced in chapter 1, establishing the study's inclusion/exclusion criteria necessitates addressing the simultaneous need to promote both sample homogeneity and sample heterogeneity. Screening criteria should promote inclusion of a group of participants experiencing same/similar disorder(s) or conditions, yet with sufficient variability on key dimensions to permit adequate testing of group difference hypotheses and generating conclusions generalizable to the population being studied (Leonard et al., 2003; Zweben et al., 1994). This may mean including participants who reflect the full range of, for example, severity in autistic symptoms; frequency of binge drinking; time since exposure to a traumatic event; readiness to change one's intimate partner violence behaviors; or degree of functional impairment as a consequence of a mental or physical health condition.

Screening as Process
Screening, however, might be designed as a two-step process. Initial or prescreening might be highly inclusive, whereas secondary screening for study eligibility might apply more stringent criteria. Fewer participants will qualify once the additional criteria are applied using this sort of "funnel" approach (Spilker & Cramer, 1992). In the end, good screening criteria exclude participants who really should not be involved in a particular intervention study. This might be because of safety, reliability, ethical, or other serious concerns. Specific exclusion criteria are justified when the intervention being studied may be inadvisable or inappropriate for certain individuals: for example, testing medications with women who may be pregnant or breastfeeding (Zweben et al., 1994). Specific criteria for exclusion are also justified when factors are likely to present study confounds or impede longitudinal participation. Examples include the exclusion of individuals with certain co-occurring problems or circumstances, such as suicidality; concurrent treatment involvement; or engagement in the criminal justice system.

In order to maximize the diversity of participants included in intervention research by minimizing the (unintentional) exclusion of participants from diverse backgrounds, certain screening strategies can be employed. For example, a multisite study of interventions to treat individuals diagnosed with alcohol dependence employed a flexible screening procedure while adhering to a set of highly structured inclusion/exclusion criteria. The flexible procedure allowed repeat screening of individuals initially deemed ineligible because of certain temporary situations (e.g., currently receiving other exclusionary treatments or short-term residential instability). While the structured criteria help preserve internal validity in a study, adaptive screening protocols can help preserve participant diversity.

Zanis (2005) addressed the issue of high participant dropout rates when recruitment is not countered with adequate screening for factors that might preclude ability to meet the study demands. Examples of personal, social, and environmental screening factors might include individuals' motivation to participate, possible intrusion of criminal sentencing, likelihood of moving away from the area, and individuals' competing life demands (e.g., working, schooling, and caring for children or other family members). A participant screening strategy that has been helpful in several of our intervention studies involves the use of a participant "roles and responsibilities" document. This document, in addition to the informed consent, describes participant study obligations in bullet-point fashion, as well as what participants can expect throughout the study's duration. In discussion with the study team, participants explore and express any concerns about their ability to meet study requirements.

Thus, it is important to consider whether or not it is preferable (1) to exclude specific individuals who may have difficulty in reliably participating in the intervention or data collection protocols, or (2) to modify data collection practices to suit their specific circumstances (e.g., allowing either telephone or mailed questionnaire data collection instead of face-to-face interviews)—especially if doing so enhances sample diversity. Using the previously mentioned "roles and responsibilities" discussion, creative problem solving can be employed to develop arrangements that facilitate an individuals' study participation. Special (IRB-approved) arrangements can include setting up evening/weekend hours, providing bus tokens or cab vouchers, allowing for flexibility in location of assessment interviews, and collaboratively problem solving other barriers. Taken together, such efforts may help to maximize participant recruitment, as well as participant retention (see chapter 3).

Palmer, Yelland, and Taft (2011) encouraged investigators to consider the impact that screening may have on the relationships that potential participants have with others. Consider, for example, an individual who screens as being eligible for participation in an intervention study for survivors of intimate partner violence. Recruitment may pose risks to that individual as a result of his or her identification of the problem and as his or her behavior begins to change through the course of intervention; these are risks beyond the immediate risks of the intervention being tested (Palmer et al., 2011; Smith & Meyers, 2004). Therefore, Palmer and colleagues (2011) encouraged investigators to conduct screening through a "narrative and relational based approach," which sees individuals as being meaningfully placed within their various contexts (p. 2).

Screening Costs

Cost efficiency is another important consideration during the screening step of the recruitment process. For example, it is especially helpful when initial prescreening can be conducted using less expensive online or telephone approaches (see Box 2.3 for a sample script to introduce a prescreening tool). Such methods can help investigators efficiently exclude clearly ineligible participants before scheduling more costly and time-intensive screening appointments, appointments that also may be intrusive for potential participants.

The least expensive and most sensitive screening procedures should be conducted first; if a person is ineligible for participation, it will become apparent early in the process. The most sensitive procedures are those that have the greatest ability to discriminate between individuals who will and will not be eligible. For example, the TimeLine FollowBack (TLFB) interview (Sobell, Maisto, Sobell, & Cooper, 1979) is a retrospective, calendar-based method for assessing an individual's recent (past 3 months) daily alcohol consumption patterns. This method allows for a relatively quick, easy, and accurate indication of whether or not a person's recent drinking behaviors meet a set of study inclusion criteria.

As a relatively simple example of cost efficiency in terms of prescreening, in a multisite study of interventions to treat alcohol dependence, 359 potential participants received telephone quick-screening at our site. Of that number, 216 potential participants progressed to the step of in-person screening, and 133 individuals ultimately were enrolled into the study. The cost efficiency of prescreening through a telephone quick-screen process is demonstrated by the fact that study resources and participant effort were saved with the early identification of 143 individuals who would not have successfully passed through the more extensive, expensive, and intrusive in-person screening step.

Box 2.3 Sample Telephone Prescreen Introduction Script

Telephone Quick Screen (TQS) Script

Thank you for inquiring about our study.

Are you calling for: **yourself** or **someone else**? **(Circle)**

> *If **someone else**—briefly explain the study (see Information Pamphlet).*
> *If **yourself**—briefly explain the study and continue with TQS.*

How did you hear about our study? _____

I will now ask you some questions to help identify your eligibility for the research study. You may consider some of the questions to be personal or sensitive in nature. I will be asking questions about your alcohol or drug use, medical history, and mental health. The information you provide is considered confidential and only research staff will have access to your protected health information.

In answering these questions, you are giving us your permission to use your answers to help us understand the individuals interested in this study. The information that you provide may be compiled with other participants' information and presented at meetings and/or published so that it can benefit others; however, no information identifiable with you will be used. Your name will be used only to contact you regarding study participation or to schedule future appointments.

Your information will also be used to make an initial determination as to whether or not you are eligible for participation in the study.

Please feel free to interrupt and ask any questions at any point. You may also stop the interview at any time if you choose to do so.

[Administer evidence-supported brief screen tools here, record responses.]

Participant Yield

The number of individuals actually enrolled in a study divided by the number who are formally screened for potential participation is called the *participant yield* (e.g., Czajkowski et al., n.d.), a key feasibility metric. Participant yield is an important indicator of the ability to appropriately recruit willing participants, as illustrated by the following case example. In preparation for a Phase III clinical research study in which a new combination of interventions was to be studied to treat individuals with bipolar disorder, prevalence data provided by the study site indicated that about 200 members of the clinic population had a current diagnosis of bipolar disorder, thus prescreening was positive for this initial study criterion because they are being treated for this problem. In the end, our study team received permission from 16 clients to be further screened for participation eligibility; in the end, only 8 were both willing and eligible for enrollment in the study. The study's protocol complexity affected clients' willingness to participate. This case demonstrates that even when adequate numbers of potential participants appear to be available, too few may be both willing and eligible to participate. This again highlights the need for sound pilot work as related to protocol acceptability and feasibility.

Recruitment Yield

By definition, *recruitment yield* is calculated as the number of individuals who agree to be formally screened divided by the number of individuals in the pool of those eligible for screening into the study. We hope to see relatively high ratios for this participant yield indicator (large numerators). Although recruitment yield is a helpful metric, we see from the bipolar treatment study example above that it is not the whole story. In that example, while the participant yield was good (8 out of 16, or a 50% yield), the size of the group initially recruited was painfully small: recruitment yield (16 out of a potential pool of 200) was only 8% (see Figure 2.5).

In chapter 4, we discuss recruitment yield effectiveness (RYE) ratios, which reflect the power of a particular recruitment method in generating enrolled participants. These ratios assist investigators in developing their recruitment budgets for staff time and costs.

Screening and Participant Motivation

Finally, screening interviews can also be motivating experiences for potential participants; the screening process can increase commitment to participate, if well managed. If mishandled, however, this step can

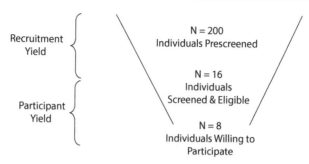

Figure 2.5 Recruitment and Participant Yield: Bipolar Intervention Study Example

also contribute to recruitment failure. For example, if potential participants feel that the information demand is too tedious, somehow demeaning, or will not be used for their own benefit, they may decide that the personal costs of participation in the study outweigh the potential gains. Screening procedures and feedback to participants may themselves affect individuals' behavior change or capture change that has already occurred prior to the onset of an intervention study; this, in turn, can affect the study's results or their interpretation (Epstein et al., 2005). Statistical methods such as baseline trajectory analysis may be a useful tool to help account for preintervention change detected through screening (see, for example, Berger, Brondino, Fisher, Gwyther, & Garbutt, 2016). The screening step is a potential participant's first, and often most significant, contact with research staff, and the encounter needs to build rapport, establish trust, and be responsive to the potential participant's aims. Remember, however, that none of the information collected during screening may be used as study data unless consent to do so has been obtained.

Consenting

The third step in developing and refining a recruitment plan is to ensure a consenting process that will promote the ethical recruitment and retention of intervention research participants. Investigators should remember, "informed consent involves both the process which is the consent dialogue and the documentation of obtaining informed consent" (CenterWatch, 2013, p. 2). Process elements for informed consent to participate in intervention studies should, at a minimum, include (list adapted from CenterWatch, 2013):

- Assessing an individual's capacity to provide consent (i.e., cognitive and legal ability);
- Presentation in an environment where the potential participant feels safe, the conversation remains private, and distractions or competing demands for attention are no more than minimal;
- A dialogue in which consent information is presented and the potential participant has ample opportunity to explore questions or concerns, and really understand what study participation will mean for themselves;
- Study personnel consistently assessing how well the potential participant understands the consent elements; and,
- Documentation of the consent process having been implemented.

Participants in intervention research often remember only portions of the information contained in informed consent; understanding the information takes us only halfway to the consent goal (Festinger, Dugosh, Croft, Arabia, & Marlowe, 2010). For example, Moodley, Pather, and Myer (2005) found that individuals from disadvantaged South African communities participating in influenza vaccine trials had a low rate of recall for having been randomly assigned to different treatments (21%) and a high rate of misinterpretation regarding the placebo being an inactive medication (81%). The authors concluded that the informed consent process used with these individuals was insufficient and in need of improvement.

Investigators engaged in the process of informed consent may also encounter potential participants who have cognitive impairments due to psychiatric disorders, dementia, or developmental disabilities that may affect their capacity to consent (Zayas, Cabassa, & Perez, 2005), and therefore should not be engaged in particular types of intervention research (e.g., research with complex performance or adherence expectations).

Elements of Consent
In order to ethically recruit appropriate individuals into intervention studies, the informed consent process should meet standards for including the elements of information, comprehension, and voluntariness (US

Department of Health and Human Services, 1978). For example, providing information about the potential or anticipated risks and benefits of an intervention should be a standard of information provided to all potential participants. In addition, consent information should be delivered in language that is developmentally and culturally appropriate, and written or spoken at the comprehension level of the potential participants. Regardless of informed consent format (e.g., written or verbal), these elements and related standards are a part of the consenting process and IRBs are responsible for assessing and monitoring their inclusion and procedures for implementation.

Consent Process

To ensure that the opportunity to participate in intervention research is maximally available and accessible to all potentially interested individuals, especially individuals from disadvantaged backgrounds, we recommend employing enhanced consent procedures. One procedure that we recommend is scheduling the initial research appointment with sufficient time devoted to the informed consent process. This includes dedicating time for potential participants to fully review the informed consent material, at their own pace, and obtain answers to any study-related questions or concerns.

Another procedure is for project staff to present participants with an overview document or brief video presentation reviewing highlights of the more detailed informed consent material. The overview guides project staff in emphasizing, discussing, and clarifying procedures and expectations with all potential participants. For example, a random assignment process can be explained in layperson language as being like the flip of a coin. Use of this strategy facilitates standardization among staff in their approach to conducting informed consent interviews. The overview document or video can also be used to review key elements of consent discussed with participants. For example, it may contain key questions, such as:

- "What do you understand about your chances of being randomly assigned to the intervention condition?"
- "How many times do you understand that you will be asked to complete assessment forms?"
- "When do you believe that you will receive the incentive payments?"

These questions allow project staff to assess and clarify potential participants' comprehension of the research process (see Box 2.4 for example text of an informed consent overview document).

In an innovative study, monetary incentives increased participants' recall of intervention research consent information: participants were paid $5.00 for each of 15 pieces of consent document information correctly recalled (Festinger et al., 2009). Quizzes are a useful tool for assessing participant comprehension and recall of consent details, as well. Potential participants can also be encouraged to take home the informed consent document prior to signing in order to discuss potential study participation with their family and friends to ensure that they are comfortable with their consent decision.

Rolling consent is yet another procedure that we routinely employ for enhancing the informed consent process. Rolling consent can be implemented in at least two different ways. First, rolling consent may include a page-by-page or item-by-item discussion of the informed consent document. Potential participants and project staff initial each item or page of the consent document, signifying that the specific contents were discussed and understood. This can be especially effective for relatively long, complex consent documents. Second, rolling consent may take the form of intermittent informed consent interviews throughout an extended period of participation in a longitudinal study. This form of rolling consent helps to remind participants of key aspects of the research enterprise, such as the voluntary nature of their participation and what to expect in the near future. This form of rolling consent has been supported, in part, by Festinger and colleagues (2010), who found that "corrected feedback" based on the responses to a "consent quiz" throughout the course of a longitudinal study improved recall of consent information. Rolling consent procedures may help to facilitate participants' trust, and thus, retention in the research. Rolling consent is also consistent with a process model of informed consent, which encourages active and continuous involvement by participants in decision-making about study participation (Lidz, Appelbaum, & Meisel, 1988). This is especially germane to the informed consent process with disadvantaged populations (Murphy et al., 2004).

Serial consent differs from rolling consent in a significant manner. Serial consent involves a complete consent process for each stage of participation in an intervention study. For example, in a jail in-reach study,

Box 2.4 Sample Informed Consent Overview Script

Overview[a] of Consent to Participate in a Research Study
University of Wisconsin-Milwaukee and
Sinai Samaritan Medical Center at Aurora Healthcare

Title of Study: Combining Medications and Behavioral Interventions for Treatment of Alcoholism

Principal Investigators: [Insert names]
Co-Investigators: [Insert names]

☐ **Sponsor**
This study is funded by the National Institute on Alcoholism and Alcohol Abuse.

☐ **Nature and Purpose of Study**
The purpose of this study is to evaluate the effectiveness of medications and behavioral therapies in the treatment of alcoholism. You will receive at least one of two types of behavioral therapy, and you will either receive both of the study medications, one of the study medications and placebo (sugar pill), placebo only (sugar pills), or you will receive no pills and only the Combined Behavioral Intervention (CBI) therapy. If you receive study pills, you will also receive the behavioral therapy of Medical Management. You will be randomly assigned to one of these treatment conditions (like the flip of a coin), which means that you could end up with medication only or possibly therapy only. *How would you feel about this?*

☐ **Duration**
The study will last about 16 months. It is important to the integrity of the study that those who start the study complete the entire 16 months. *Do you think you can commit to that length of time?*

☐ **Procedures**
☐ You will be asked questions about your alcohol use, your well-being, and you and your family's history of mental and physical health problems. You will be asked to perform or complete Breathalyzer tests, blood draws, submit urine specimens, and to have a physical exam including an Electrocardiogram (ECG) if clinically indicated.

☐ If assigned to a medication treatment assignment, neither you nor the treating professionals will know what combination of medications and/ or placebo you are taking until the end of the study.

☐ You will be required to come to the clinic at least once a week at the beginning and less frequently towards the end of treatment. *Do you think you can make that commitment?*

[a] Note that this is not a complete informed consent document; it is an example of building an overview script with prompts to check participant comprehension.

participants first provided consent to engage in the addiction severity brief screening process, as these results would serve two functions: one was to establish whether the women met inclusion criteria, the other helped address one of the study questions. Thus, information gathered during the screening phase could become data. Subsequently, the women were randomly assigned to one of the intervention conditions being compared: thus, they engaged in a second phase of consent about the intervention stage to which they had been only alerted during the first stage consent process.

Enrollment

The fourth and final step in developing and refining a recruitment plan is to consider the impact that the recruitment process may have on an individual's willingness to enroll and remain in an intervention research study. Intervention research often engages populations that are difficult to enroll and retain. Some examples include populations whose members are vulnerable or disenfranchised by virtue of race/ethnicity, immigrant/refugee status, disability, mental disorder, homelessness, sexual orientation, or experiences of discrimination and oppression. In many cases, extraordinary efforts need to be developed to enroll and retain a sufficient and diversified sample from these populations. Leonard et al. (2003) described structural, motivational, and behavioral efforts associated with the successful recruitment/enrollment and retention of intervention research participants from underserved and HIV-affected populations.

A critical group that is sometimes especially difficult and expensive to enroll and retain in intervention research is an appropriate control group (Schechter & Lebovitch, 2005). Furthermore, it is sometimes difficult to avoid the problem of control group contamination when some of the control group participants come into contact and interact with participants in the intervention group. For example, one of our study teams had to turn away an individual eligible and wishing to enroll in a medication trial for treatment of an alcohol use disorder. The problem: his spouse was already enrolled and randomly assigned to a (double-blind) medication condition. The risk was too great that either spouse could accidentally (or intentionally) take the other's active or placebo medication, thereby confounding the results.

Enrollment Timeliness

Intervention research teams should seek to minimize the time lag between their participants' first efforts to engage the study services and becoming enrolled; this includes being mindful of when participants are first engaged to complete consent and study assessment measures, and also minimizing any delay between assessment and the start of intervention activities. Minimizing this time period and the number of impediments experienced by potential participants may reduce unnecessary participant attrition due to loss of interest, frustration, or securing services elsewhere (Hinshaw et al., 2004). For example, ensuring immediate appointment availability can help to expedite eligible participants' enrollment into an intervention study. Appointment availability reduces potential participants' wait for an appointment and may eliminate the need for individuals to be placed on waiting lists, where attrition may easily occur. Immediate scheduling may also increase the chances that potential participants will attend their appointments because it capitalizes on their immediate interest and attention. In the same vein, the availability of intervention research staff to answer individuals' phone calls and respond to phone or e-mail messages may enhance participation by minimizing frustration with hard-to-reach study personnel. These accessibility strategies should be used throughout an intervention study, as they are responsive and establish a climate of helpfulness.

Incentives to Participate

Finally, we would be remiss in failing to mention the role of incentive payments in the enrollment of study participants. Incentive payments have been linked to greater enrollment, appointment adherence, and reduced attrition in behavioral intervention research studies (e.g., DiClemente & Wingood, 1998; Kamb et al., 1998; Post, Cruz, & Harman, 2006). Although payment of incentives to participants is practiced widely, there are many different perspectives on the ethics and utility of such practices (Johnson & Remien, 2003; Seddon, 2005). This is especially true when discussing payment for completion of study assessment measures (the research portion) versus payment for participation in the intervention or treatment programs being tested (Johnson & Remien, 2003). In our experience, payment for completing assessment measures is of value in recruiting participants.

An important recruitment aspect of the incentives debate revolves around amounts that are meaningful without being coercive. Influences of incentive payments on participant enrollment may vary by context, target population, and type of incentive offered (e.g., monetary—cash, gift certificates, or gift cards—and nonmonetary, material goods or services). There are no clear-cut methods or standards for determining appropriate amounts or levels of incentives offered in a study (Seddon, 2005). Investigators need to consider the nature of the research (e.g., level of time, effort, inconvenience), study population (i.e., for the targeted group, what would be sufficiently rewarding without being coercive), geographical location and relative cost of living, and principles that guide the ethical conduct of research activities. These issues are examined in greater detail in chapter 3.

CHAPTER SUMMARY

The recruitment of participants largely drives the success of any intervention study. Investigators, however, often overestimate the number of eligible individuals who may be willing to participate in intervention research. The ultimate goal of recruitment processes is to engage sufficient numbers of participants who adequately represent the target population. This, in turn, allows intervention research findings to be more informative because of increased generalizability. Thus, although an intervention study may have a sound research design, the study may not be able to generate the data needed to confidently test study hypotheses. The process and methods of recruitment in intervention research presented in this chapter maximize the success of investigators in recruiting participants while upholding scientifically and ethically responsible strategies. Finally, there is a symbiotic relationship between participant recruitment and retention. That is, if recruitment is done well, in that potential participants are treated with respect and dignity, a good foundation has been laid for retention. Participant retention in intervention research is the subject of the next chapter.

3

Participant Retention

Participant retention is central to social work behavioral intervention and evaluation research studies that employ longitudinal, repeated measurement designs and those requiring multiple episodes of data collection. In 2004, a working group published a research recruitment and retention analysis in which they observed that, once participants are successfully recruited, "their retention throughout the investigation is essential for ensuring valid findings, particularly in the case of long-term treatment research or prospective longitudinal studies" (Hinshaw et al., 2004, p. 1038). Poor retention of study participants in behavioral intervention studies is considered to be unfortunately common among published reports (Toerien et al., 2009).

The purpose of this chapter is to present ideas that will help investigators develop strategic participant retention plans, drawn from literature in multiple disciplines and from the authors' practical experiences. This chapter extends content introduced in chapters 1 and 2, and prepares a foundation for some of the tools and resources discussed in chapter 4. The first part of this chapter addresses the significance of participant retention and attrition, issues regarding disproportionate attrition, intervention versus study attrition, the high cost of attrition, how retention and attrition might be operationalized, how retention might be measured (metrics), determining reasonable retention rates, and patterns in the timing of attrition. The second part of this chapter presents a variety of challenges to successful participant retention (participant characteristics, goodness-of-fit with intervention components and with the study protocol). Finally, the chapter concludes with a discussion of retention techniques and strategies for enhancing participant retention.

SIGNIFICANCE OF PARTICIPANT RETENTION AND ATTRITION

As noted in chapter 1, recruitment efforts lead to participants deciding to enroll in a study, whereas retention efforts contribute to their remaining engaged through the conclusion of a study (Voyer, Lauzon, Collin, & O'Brien, 2008). While recruitment efforts are necessary to ensure scientific integrity, their implementation is not sufficient: specific efforts are needed to ensure that sufficient numbers and diversity of participants also are retained over time. Statistical power concerns, such as those discussed by Prinz et al. (2001), were introduced in chapters 1 and 2. Also as noted in chapter 1, two apparently reciprocal terms emerge in literature concerning participant retention in research studies: *promoting retention* appears to be treated in the same manner as *reducing attrition*, and the concept of *dropout* appears to be handled in the same manner as *attrition* (e.g., Davis, Brome, & Cox, 2002).

Disproportionate Attrition

In addition to study integrity threats, another major consequence of participant attrition from intervention and evaluation studies warrants close attention. This is the possibility that participant attrition might occur disproportionately, in a nonrandom or an otherwise systematic fashion, across intervention or key demographic groups (Cotter, Burke, Loeber, & Navratil, 2002). Thus, retained participants may no longer adequately represent their relevant subgroups in the population, or for that matter, the subgroups initially engaged in the study. For example, attrition may occur differentially among participants with different types of diagnoses (e.g., solo versus co-occurring conditions), from differing demographic groups (e.g., men versus women, younger versus older adults, white versus black adolescents), or based on the nature of their past experiences with treatment (first versus multiple attempts).

Disproportionate attrition from different study subgroups represents a major source of threat to both internal and external validity of a study's findings. *Internal validity* is potentially threatened when differential or uneven attrition occurs between the compared groups, because differences in observed outcomes cannot confidently be attributed to the interventions; differences among those who were retained in the compared groups may just as easily explain the observed differences (Braver & Smith, 1996; Ribisl et al., 1996). For example, Lauby et al. (1996) observed that individuals most at risk of HIV exposure by virtue of engaging in drug misuse also were the least likely to be retained over the course of a longitudinal study. Uneven attrition between randomized groups impacts the study's internal validity. And, participant attrition seldom occurs in a random fashion (Hinshaw et al., 2004; Ribisl et al., 1996). As noted by Bell et al. (2008), "A study that starts and ends with 100 (representative) retained cases is more convincing than a study that starts with 500 (equally representative) cases but only successfully retains 100 or even 200 cases" (p. 332).

External validity is threatened when individuals who have participated throughout the entire study period are no longer representative of the population from which they were initially drawn, or they differ meaningfully from the participants lost through attrition. In other words, generalizability of the study results becomes limited (Braver & Smith, 1996; Ribisl et al., 1996). For example, Winslow et al. (2009) discussed an external validity threat inherent in many parenting education research studies. Poor retention of families with children experiencing or at risk of developing mental health, educational, or social relationship problems limits the usefulness of the intervention studies: these are the very families for which the interventions could potentially have the greatest impact.

Intervention Versus Study Attrition

It is important to recall the distinction between participants dropping out of the intervention versus dropping out of the study (e.g., Stasiewicz & Stalker, 1999). On the surface, this may appear to be a minor case of semantics. However, when more carefully examined, a meaningful difference emerges between *intervention attrition* and *attrition from research data collection* (Lauby et al., 1996). Behavioral intervention study designers must address participants' ability to accomplish all requirements of the intervention being tested and their willingness to complete the intervention protocol. On the other hand, investigators also need to design the research components in such a way that participants are interested in and capable of completing all data collection procedures. These concepts of intervention and study retention are clearly intertwined, positively and negatively, in that participants' experiences with intervention protocols affect their willingness to participate in the data collection components, and vice versa. And, as noted in chapter 2, their experiences with the recruitment process also have an impact on their retention or attrition.

The High Cost of Attrition

The study costs associated with each participant lost to follow-up can be extremely high relative to costs associated with a carefully executed participant retention plan. In a multisite alcohol treatment study, the average direct cost to recruit each participant at one site was about $445 using newspaper and radio advertisements. An additional estimated $400 per person was added in the expense of staff members' time and clinical lab tests essential in screening and enrolling eligible study participants (Berger et al., 2013). Thus, the loss of any enrolled participant became quite expensive, especially as incentive payments were made along the way.

Similarly, a 1-year period of recruitment into a randomized controlled trial of an intervention for women with HIV sexual exposure risk and co-occurring substance use disorders resulted in 202 referrals for the study. Of this number, 53 women proceeded to study enrollment, with an average recruitment cost of $293.48 per enrolled participant. Some recruitment methods, such as bus ads and targeted mailings, required extensive additional expense compared to other methods, such as the use of flyers and word-of-mouth, and had lower rates of referrals that "made it through" to study enrollment compared to the less expensive methods (Blaeser et al., 2008). Once again, the cost of losing any one enrolled participant is high; furthermore, losing participants disproportionately from either the new intervention or treatment as usual group would jeopardize the study results. Or, investigators need to spend additional recruitment effort, time, and dollars to recruit replacement participants.

Therefore, in study planning it is important to weigh recruitment and retention costs against the costs of losing participants (Cotter, Burke, Stouthamer-Loeber, & Loeber, 2005); costs associated with retention efforts may be the lesser of the two (see chapter 4 for more details). And, it is important to establish a process for regularly monitoring and assessing retention and attrition throughout the entire study period so that adjustments can be made as necessary—waiting until the end of the study period leaves investigators with few options for addressing retention issues.

OPERATIONALIZING PARTICIPANT RETENTION

The way that participant retention and attrition are operationalized in a particular intervention study has profound implications for how these constructs are measured. Most simply, participant retention could be treated as a dichotomous variable: whether or not a participant completed all of the intervention and study components. In this case, investigators can compute retention rate (RR) and Attrition Rate (AR) in terms of the ratio of the number of participants retained through completion (N_C) divided by the number of participants initially recruited and enrolled (N_{IE}):

$$RR = N_C / N_{IE}$$

$$AR = 100\% \text{ minus } RR$$

For example, imagine that 50 families were initially enrolled in a 6-month child welfare intervention study comparing the outcomes of home versus office visits (25 families randomly assigned to each condition). At the end of 6 months, 12 families had dropped out of the study, leaving 38 families (50 minus 12). Study retention would include the 38 who completed the study divided by the original sample size of 50: thus, we have a 76% *retention rate* (RR), or 24% *attrition rate* (AR = 100% minus 76%).

Examining the overall retention rate may not suffice, however, since the rate may differ across the intervention groups being compared. Furthermore, there may be important distinctions even within an intervention group. Braver and Smith (1996) describe a hypothetical example in which equal proportions of individuals drop out of two treatment conditions, with attrition in one treatment group occurring primarily among participants experiencing the greatest degree of impairment, while in the other group attrition is highest among participants experiencing lesser degrees of impairment. Despite equivalent attrition rates for the two groups, study results comparing outcomes for the two groups would either over- or underrepresent the impact of the intervention because of the nonrandom pattern of attrition. Thus, assessments of retention or attrition may need to include greater complexity than a simple dichotomous indicator of completion might allow.

Greater Complexity

Participant retention may be operationalized as a more complex, dimensional variable indicating the proportion of the intervention (also called *dose*) received by each participant. For example, retention can be defined as the number of days an individual participated in the intervention divided by the total number of days that participation was possible (Mann, Lehert, & Morgan, 2004). Attrition occurring between the time of study enrollment and the initiation of intervention may need to be counted when calculating dropout rates. It is not uncommon that individuals who engaged in an intake or baseline assessment session do not return for even the first of the planned intervention sessions, especially if the study assessment is lengthy or complicated (see *participant burden*, discussed later in this chapter). This becomes relevant in light of the observation by David et al. (2013), who detected significant differences in study attrition rates as a function of intervention dose received with participants in a prison prerelease intervention (or control group). Participants receiving the full-dose intervention had the lowest postrelease follow-up attrition rate (10.3%). The highest attrition rate was observed among those receiving only a partial dose of the prison-based intervention (86.4%). The nonintervention control group had an attrition rate of 26.8%. Perhaps individuals whose circumstances interfered with receiving the full-dose intervention are people for whom postrelease instability and crises continue to interfere with study participation. Thus, participants retained in the study are no longer fully representative of the population initially enrolled.

Behavioral intervention researchers also may wish to measure aspects of *treatment adherence* and *level of participation*, as opposed to attendance alone: participants may show up for all scheduled activities, yet their degree of engagement in the intervention or data collection sessions may vary. For example, one (precontemplation) statement rated by participants using a 5-point scale of agreement on our team's *Safe At Home* instrument for assessing readiness to change intimate partner violence is: "I'll come to groups, but I won't talk." Attendance may not be a sufficient indicator of intervention exposure and engagement.

RETENTION METRICS

We have seen that losing even a few study participants can reduce an already small sample to an unproductive level. But it is not easy to determine what a reasonable retention goal might be for every intervention study, nor is it easy to predict likely rates of study attrition. These estimates, however, are crucial planning tools for achieving minimum sample sizes determined through power analysis (see chapter 4).

Research funding requirements may dictate strong retention rates for preventive and treatment intervention studies: the Substance Abuse and Health Services Administration (SAMHSA) has set the bar at 80% retention, for example. Meyers, Webb, Frantz, and Randall (2003), in their literature review, reported retention rates for substance use studies ranging from 40% to 98%, and adolescent studies in the 36%–98% range. Scott's (2004) review states, "The general rule of thumb, to get at least 70%, has come under increasing criticism for leaving open the door to biases that are as large or larger than the treatment effects being sought" (p. 30). This point is further demonstrated in the differing study conclusions drawn from data that Scott (2004) presented comparing results of studies at points where 70% versus 90%–100% of the studies' samples were complete—in some cases, different conclusions would be drawn.

Determining Reasonable Retention Rates

In their meta-analysis of studies testing the efficacy of the medication acamprosate combined with psychosocial intervention for the treatment of alcohol dependence, Mann, Lehert, and Morgan (2004) noted that study attrition rates varied from 22% to 71% (averaging 51%) across 17 studies involving a total of 4,087 participants. Attrition rates in the 40%–53% range are not unusual in substance use, homelessness, and child mental health studies (Ribisl et al., 1996). It is important to review how retention rates were calculated in a particular study. For example, Cepeda and Valdez (2010) computed a 12-month follow-up rate of 98% in two waves of a longitudinal, community-based study of blood-borne and sexually transmitted infection rates among a group of 300 Mexican American individuals who used heroin. While this high rate of retention is admirable, it is important to note that the denominator in their calculations excluded individuals who withdrew from the study or were deceased. A more conservative analysis, using the full 300 in the denominator, leads to a (still admirable) retention rate of 91%.

Literature reviewed by Hansten, Downey, Rosengren, and Donovan (2000) suggest that studies in the 65%–80% range of retention should not be discounted simply on the basis of methodological concerns, especially if the investigators can demonstrate a lack of significant differences among those retained and those lost to follow-up. However, we caution that differences would need to be assessed on a range of potentially relevant variables, including but not limited to participant demographic, diagnosis/assessment, problem severity, and other potentially discriminating characteristics—just because no differences were found on the variables measured does not mean that no differences exist. Furthermore, with small sample sizes, assessing the effect of multiple participant characteristic variables on study retention/attrition may be complicated or compromised.

Winslow et al. (2009) emphasize recruitment and retention analyses based on examining variables with a logical relationship to the intervention under study. Specific to intervention with divorced families, they found intervention timing to be a key factor in predicting participant retention: the closer to the time of divorce that enrollment occurred, the greater the likelihood of retention. That is, the authors conducted logistic regression on a group of 52 families who enrolled but never attended versus those who dropped out after the first session. This valuable analysis was permissible only because the investigators had the foresight to collect these data from individuals who elected not to participate or dropped out of the intervention study prior to completion.

Attrition Patterns

Not only does attrition occur in a nonrandom fashion but also it does not happen in a linear fashion over time, either. The pattern of retention rates following screening and randomization for an alcohol treatment study are presented in Figure 3.1. A large number of participants were lost initially, between screening and baseline measurement (Berger et al., 2013), compared to later in the study.

Similarly, BootsMiller et al. (1998) described an uneven retention pattern characterized by great initial attrition followed by diminishing attrition over the course of their longitudinal study of individuals dually diagnosed with mental disorders and substance misuse (see Figure 3.2).

Over 25 years ago, a meta-analysis of preventive interventions in substance abuse was published to help inform other investigators; the report summarized attrition results across 85 longitudinal studies (Hansen, Tobler, & Graham, 1990). The authors concluded that attrition increased with time from pretest/baseline, and that attrition rates were highest early in the study: on average, 21.7% were lost during the first 6 months. Although attrition rates declined at subsequent periods, attrition continued to occur: averaging across the 85 studies, a total of 26.6% had been lost at 1 year and 28.2% at 2 years following pretest/baseline measurement. Therefore, it is important for investigators

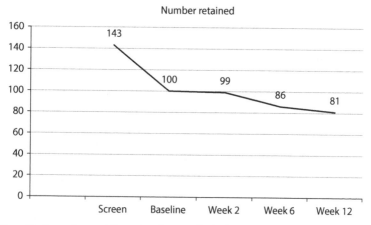

Figure 3.1 Screening and Retention Rates: Alcohol Treatment Study (Berger et al., 2013)

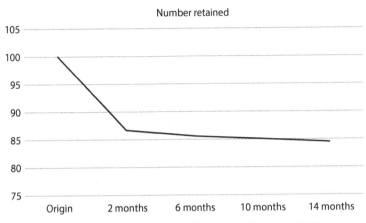

Figure 3.2 Study Retention Rates Reported by BootsMiller et al. (2008)

who plan behavioral intervention studies to take into consideration
attrition trends across time, and not simply overall retention/attrition
rates. Investigators would do well to strategically and continuously
apply Institutional Review Board (IRB)-approved, tailored procedures
for the prevention of participant attrition throughout the course of an
intervention study.

RETENTION CHALLENGES

Social work and behavioral scientists frequently engage in intervention
studies involving "sensitive topics and study populations vulnerable on
multiple fronts who are difficult to retain" over time (Kavanaugh, Moro,
Savage, & Mehendale, 2006, p. 244). We may be engaging in studies
with individuals experiencing cognitive and other participation barriers associated with traumatic brain injury, spinal cord injury, or stroke,
for example (Bell et al., 2008). Or, our studies may include survivors of
intimate partner violence whose experiences of housing, safety, income
or employment instability, and major life transitions may interfere with
their continued participation in longitudinal research studies (Clough
et al., 2011). In many instances, we are working with individuals from
stigmatized, "highly marginalized and hidden" population groups, and
individuals who engage in socially sensitive, undesirable, or stigmatized

behaviors (Cepeda & Valdez, 2010, p. 700). Some of the factors contributing to study retention difficulties include "high residential mobility, homelessness, death, disability, illegal activities, incarceration, residence in mental health or substance abuse treatment agencies, lack of telephone or driver's license, illiteracy, aliases, name changes, false locator data, and unreliable information from contacts" (Passetti et al., 2000, p. 196).

An example drawn from our experiences, and observed by others (David, Alati, Ware & Kinner, 2013; Goshin & Byrne, 2012), involves difficulties with tracking incarcerated individuals during community reentry. These difficulties may arise from a host of complicating factors: uncertain release dates, reincarceration events, uncertain addresses and contact numbers, suspicion among members of the individuals' social networks, and stigmatized reasons for being involved in the intervention research. Similarly, Meyers, Webb, Frantz, and Randall (2002) reported that adolescent study participants requiring the greatest effort in tracking also were those having the greatest degree of behavioral and substance use problems at 6-month follow-up. The need for residential treatment placement of these adolescents, or any study's participants, may impede study follow-up with those participants (Yetarian et al., 2012). Residential instability or alienation from family and friends, "social disaffiliation," may accentuate study attrition, as well (Scott, 2004, p. 22). As a result, without sufficient retention effort, intervention studies may become biased in favor of individuals who are doing well, losing that part of the picture that should be contributed by individuals whose experiences are not as positive.

Like others, Nemes et al. (2002) reported that the most easily retained study participants were those who had completed the treatment protocol, and Walton et al. (1998) reported the greatest difficulties with participants who had the poorest treatment outcomes. Thus, in these situations with poor participant retention we may erroneously conclude that our intervention is more effective than it actually is. On the other hand, we may lose the picture provided by people who become disinterested once they are doing well; retaining a disproportionate number of those who continue to struggle leads us to erroneously conclude that our intervention is less effective than it might actually be.

Retention challenges affect intervention studies involving children and adolescents, pregnant women, older adults, individuals and families at risk of becoming homeless, refugees, individuals experiencing serious mental disorder or who are abusing substances, and others whose complicated lives prohibit regular participation in regimented intervention and research activities. Investigators need to think creatively about approaches for preventing participant attrition in behavioral intervention studies. It helps to think about some of the factors known to contribute to attrition.

Participant Characteristics

A number of studies report statistical associations between participant-specific variables and patterns of study attrition. For example, members of some racial and ethnic groups may be more difficult than others to retain in intervention studies as a result of historical discrimination patterns, histories of research exploitation, and prior personal histories of negative interactions with health or human service delivery systems (Armistead et al., 2004; Shavers, Lynch, & Burmeister, 2002). Furthermore, disparities in incarceration rates across racial and ethnic groups may contribute to systematic rather than random study attrition patterns (Wang et al., 2014). Older adult participants and those dependent on public transportation may be less available during inclement weather seasons. The ability of children and adolescents to participate may be dependent on the consistency of parents' or guardians' commitment to bring them. Individuals affected by physical and cognitive impairments related to acute or chronic health conditions may experience additional obstacles to reliable study participation (Bell et al., 2008). Busy work and family roles, greater severity of behavioral health problems, and again, specific sociodemographic characteristics also represent common themes in published analyses of participant attrition. For example, Cottler et al. (1996) found that among several participant characteristic variables in their 18-month study of individuals at risk for HIV exposure related to substance misuse, only (un)employment status was significantly different between their most versus less difficult to reach study participants.

Characteristics relevant to retention and attrition may be study-specific. For example, holding negative views about healthcare influenced attrition from a study involving parents of infants with cardiac risk factors (Moser, Dracup, & Doering, 2000). In a Latino smoking cessation study, Lee and colleagues (2010) found that individuals' pre-intervention endorsement of more pros versus cons about smoking predicted greater attrition. Greater drug use severity and being female were associated with poorer retention in a family intervention study for individuals with co-occurring substance use and severe mental disorders (Mueser et al., 2009). Individuals with the least initial symptomology and most co-occurring mental health problems had the highest attrition from an Internet-delivered intervention for insomnia (Hebert, Vincent, Lewycky, & Walsh, 2010). And, in a correctional setting study of the therapeutic community approach to substance abuse treatment, investigators determined that individuals with greater levels of hostility had higher treatment group dropout rates than did individuals with lower hostility (Hiller, Knight, Saum, & Simpson, 2006).

Goodness-of-Fit with Intervention Components

Williams and colleagues (2008) pointed out that participant characteristics associated with study attrition may be difficult to change, but study characteristics may be modified to improve retention over time. For example, retention rates improve when study sites employ specialized staff dedicated to study retention activities, and when participants have positive experiences with staff and appointment processes. Carefully considering and pilot testing interventions for feasibility, adequacy, and appropriateness in application with the populations engaged in efficacy or effectiveness research are components of a wise retention plan.

Positive, early treatment response to the tested interventions may help counter participant dropout in those groups receiving the most effective treatments, while treatment failure may contribute to greater study attrition in other study conditions; attrition in nontreatment control groups may be higher than in groups receiving treatment (Mann, Lehert, & Morgan, 2004). Reasons why participants "quit" intervention studies are reflected in statements about the intervention not having the degree of impact they had hoped for (inadequate treatment response), difficulties with side effects from the intervention, loss of confidence about the wisdom of participating in research studies, actually achieving their treatment goals (thereby feeling they no longer need the intervention), participation fatigue (burden of ongoing participation is greater than they initially anticipated), or feeling like an unwelcomed member in group-based intervention (Mann, Lehert, & Morgan, 2004).

Group-based interventions potentially contribute an additional source of participant dropout: depending on a participant's characteristics and behaviors in the group situation, the individual may be made to feel more or less welcome as a member. For example, individuals who departed from a therapeutic community intervention could be differentiated from those who completed the program on the basis of personality characteristics that were less amenable to the intervention's orientation—such as the impact of dominating individuals who monopolize the group discussion (McMahon, Kelley, & Kouzekanani, 1993).

Hinshaw et al. (2004) offer recommendations to preemptively address retention barriers that derive from problems of fit between participants and the interventions under study. These recommendations include (1) participant education that is truly responsive to the consumer's interests and needs for information, as well as being culturally and developmentally relevant; (2) high-quality, explicit information about what to do in response to side effect and/or inadequate treatment response issues that may arise; (3) presenting referral resources and providing case management for participants who experience difficulties; and (4) providing participants with individualized feedback on their assessment results at the end of the study.

Goodness-of-Fit with the Study Protocol

In addition to the intervention elements, participant retention can be affected by a number of research-related issues, including but not limited to the study length and study demands. It is useful to consider the nature of fit (or lack thereof) between individual participants and study protocols. For example, in a feasibility study of approaches to treating alcohol dependence, investigators were pleased that participants randomized to a behavioral treatment (nonmedication) condition were retained at equivalent rates to participants who received medication along with behavioral treatment (The COMBINE Study Research Group, 2003). This finding was important because some recruited participants initially emphasized an interest in being assigned to medication groups.

The participant-study interface also concerns the ways in which study protocols address participants' ambivalence about their participation in the interventions and the research. Behavioral health professionals increasingly demonstrate an awareness and understanding of the role that ambivalence plays in a person's willingness to engage in intervention and motivation to make difficult behavior changes (Hohman, 2012; Wahab, 2005). At least two reports indicate that retention in treatment studies is positively related to participants' motivation to change, and that treatment ambivalence should be addressed early in the study protocol (Brocato & Wagner, 2008; Roffman, Klepsch, Wetz, Simpson, & Stephens, 1993). As a simple example, at intake to one of our substance abuse intervention studies, participants wrote themselves a letter about why they wanted to engage in the intervention; if a participant's commitment waned later in the intervention, the letter could be mailed along with information concerning ways to reengage with the study.

This motivational awareness issue presents a dilemma: recruiting individuals who already are motivated for change increases the likelihood of their retention throughout the course of the study, but this also is tantamount to "creaming" the sample—skimming off the top of the pool those who are most likely to succeed in the intervention protocol, leaving the others unstudied. As pressure increases to recruit into studies people who are not necessarily motivated to change (and thus more representative of the population and to whom results are then more generalizable), addressing ambivalence about participation in the study interventions becomes more important. This may become even more important to consider as the state of intervention science moves toward interventions that concurrently address multiple, co-occurring issues—participants may be unevenly interested in addressing each set of issues. Addressing individuals' reluctance or ambivalence to continue participating in a study that was initially of interest to them may need to be managed on a "case-by-case" basis (Cotter et al., 2002).

RETENTION TECHNIQUES

Previous literature examining participant retention provides readers with several "tricks of the trade" for improving participant retention in longitudinal intervention research (Bell et al., 2008; Boys et al., 2003; Cepeda & Valdez, 2010; Davis, Broome, & Cox, 2002; Desmond et al., 1995; Garner, Passetti, Orndorff, & Godley, 2007; Lauby et al., 1996; Pappas, Werch, & Carlson, 1998; Ribisl et al., 1996; Stanford et al., 2003; Taylor, 2009; Vander Stoep, 1999; Voyer, 2008; Winslow, Bonds, Wolchik, Sandler, & Braver, 2009). Cited recommendations can be categorized as follows (Boys et al., 2003; Davis, Broome, & Cox, 2002; Ribisl et al., 1996):

- collect locator data from participants;
- use IRB-approved locator resources (e.g., updated versions of searchable databases described by Passetti et al., 2000);
- establish a nonstigmatizing, recognizable project identity;
- prepare and motivate staff for retention activities;
- monitor and solve attrition problems throughout the course of study;
- make study participation convenient, rewarding, and meaningful;
- conduct preliminary tests of all study procedures;
- apply greatest effort early, when attrition rates are highest; and,
- customize data collection and retention efforts.

Studies using larger numbers of retention strategies representing multiple themes have been found to be more likely to retain participants at a higher rate compared to studies utilizing only a few strategies (Robinson, Dennison, Wayman, Pronovost, & Needham, 2007). In addition to these nine important recommendations, additional options warrant consideration.

Rapport/Relationship with Participants

Retention begins at recruitment, with the building of rapport between a potential participant and the intervention study. In their study involving adolescents who used substances and ran away from home, Patton et al. (2011) reported that retention decreased as a function of the number of research assistant changes involved in the participants' 24-month relationship with the study: as research assistant turnover increased, retention significantly declined.

Crucial to rapport are the establishment and maintenance of participants' trust. Similarly, nurturing trust relationships within communities is a critical aspect of research. In studies that engage ethnically diverse communities, this can be enhanced by ensuring representativeness of community among the research staff and advisory boards (Armistead et al., 2004; Hinshaw et al., 2004). Literature about community-based participatory research (CBPR) addresses many such activities.

Andersen (2007) argued the value of "relational engagement" strategies for participant retention, over and above the application of conventional retention strategies. Relational engagement involves efforts to learn about and respond to participants' values and beliefs about participating in the research, their emotional experience of participation, and their own knowledge gained through participation. Similarly, social exchange principles are offered as a guiding principle to maintain participant retention by applying open, honest communications about intervention and study expectations, and motivating participants through enjoyable personal contacts with members of the research team (McGregor, Parker, LeBlanc, & King, 2010). This represents a key opportunity to apply qualitative research methods for informing the development of quantitative studies regarding retention strategies. Additionally, throughout the duration of an intervention study, qualitative methodology can help address participant responsiveness as related to investigator identity, role, trustworthiness, attitudes, and power relationships with participants (Taylor, 2009).

In any form of longitudinal intervention or evaluation research, establishing quality relationships with participants provides a foundation for their retention; any and all interactions can either facilitate retention or increase the possibility of attrition. Careful attention must be paid to each aspect of study interactions, including tone of voice and message content, as well as non-verbal cues. Cultural relevance of these elements must also be considered. In their report concerning research involving college students, Berry and Bass (2012) discuss the importance of the generational norms and preferences of a study population in determining both data collection and participant retention strategies. They found that students prefer retention efforts that employ electronic means (e-mail, text messages, Facebook) to telephone and US mail approaches.

Knowing the populations with whom we work is critical to establishing effective, respectful interactions and working relationships with study participants (see for example Wilcox et al., 2001). Analogous is the importance of therapeutic alliance in clinical relationships: in intervention studies, it may be critical to enhance connectedness between interventionists and study participants, as well as between data collectors and participants. Brocato and Wagner (2008) found that retention in their intervention study was positively related to a measure of therapeutic alliance. Hinshaw et al. (2004) also recommended training research and intervention staff in culturally competent and respectful communication practices in relating with study participants.

Another issue is the need to consider possible geographic divides between where participants come from and the locus of research activities (Hinshaw et al., 2004). Significant barriers to ongoing study participation may derive from participants' physical, psychological, social, and emotional access to the locations where research activities take place. Several of our studies involved research activities in office locations that provided participants with ease of access: public transportation, parking, and neighborhood familiarity.

Equally important in facilitating study retention is conducting intervention research activities in nonstigmatizing locales, such as general, primary care locations rather than clinics with stigmatized specialties, or working out of locations with "social" or "education" identities, rather than "treatment" identities. In their list of 10 steps for retaining study participants, Desmond et al. (1995) included being prepared to conduct follow-up interviews wherever participants are located and willing to engage in the interview. In one study of prisoners' community reentry experiences, many of our participants preferred to schedule their interviews in community public libraries rather than at their probation and parole offices. In our study of batterer treatment programs, participants often chose interview locations within their own ethnic neighborhoods rather than locations convenient to centrally located treatment programs. Adolescents in another team's study often preferred interviews in fast-food restaurants to telephone interviews at home, for reasons of privacy from family members overhearing their responses (Meyers, Webb, Frantz, & Randall, 2002). Still others, like participants in our prospective study of women living in urban housing developments, may wish to be interviewed in research offices to be reassured of the confidentiality of the information they provide. Providing participants with options may enhance their retention in study activities. However, it is important to initially secure IRB approval for engaging in research activities at each of the multiple sites.

Participants' perceptions of themselves as being integral and valued members of the study can also increase retention. This might include facilitating social connections between participants in group interventions and involving community members in developing the identity, name, and logo for a study. In an older adults' physical activity study, Voyer et al. (2008) created a sense of community among study participants by having participants wear project logo T-shirts during study activities, having participants determine incidental intervention elements (e.g., music to be played), verbally and personally acknowledging their attendance at intervention sessions, providing "merit" awards for best attendance, and celebrating intervention milestones. Investigators also attended other social events at the participants' residential facility to become familiar with participants before the study began.

In several instances, we have conducted community-based studies in which we held focus groups prior to the start of recruitment. Participants in these groups were key informants in the communities from which we were going to recruit for the main study. Groups developed shared identity and recruitment themes for the study, and created the study name and logo based on that theme. Their ideas appeared on "branded" items given as incentives (e.g., project t-shirts). These focus group sessions have been instrumental in helping create a study identity that resonates for participants, further increasing the perceived value of study participation. These elements assist in enhancing retention, as long as there are not concerns about stigma from study involvement.

Another factor related to participant retention is the extent to which a study's staffing and administrative structures can manage the activity flow and remain responsive to participants. For example, if participant telephone calls are answered by automated systems, participants' calls are not returned promptly, or the schedule of study appointments is too full to easily accommodate new participants, they may feel frustrated and less inclined to maintain the relationship. BootsMiller et al. (1998) summarized this point in their statement: "Make participation enjoyable and effortless for participants" (p. 2678).

Participant Tracking and Maintaining Contact

The literature contains references to the importance of establishing effective systems for tracking participants over time using information collected at the time of initial recruitment and establishing a pattern of frequent contacts between study sessions (Taylor, 2009). Tracking systems should include a set of standardized procedures for documenting the research team's contact efforts: dates and times of calls, when and where reminders were sent, and records of the results of these efforts (e.g., left message, letter returned undeliverable, etc.). Computerized spreadsheets and calendar systems can be a tremendous aide in this process, delivering "ticklers" as to when a participant is due for a reminder call, letter, text, or e-mail message. In a systematic review of 21 longitudinal studies, the most commonly reported strategies for retaining study participants were highly intentional systems for contact and scheduling (Robinson, et al., 2007).

Depending on the population, identifying multiple, diverse types of informants may be advisable. On their participant locator forms, Cepeda and Valdez (2010) included full contact information for "at least one stable relative (i.e., grandparent, aunt, uncle, etc.)," and a staff member confirmed each telephone number before the participant left the baseline interview site (p. 704). In a study of individuals engaged in a longitudinal substance abuse treatment study, providing three or more informants appeared to be a critical factor, among others, in predicting study completion (Claus, Kindleberger, & Dugan, 2002). In one prisoner community reentry study, we asked participants to identify up to six individuals who would be able to assist in locating them following their release. We found that the value-added limit was reached after three informants—having more than this was not of benefit and the participants had difficulty recalling contact details for more, but having three was more helpful than having one or two. The highest rate of lost-to-follow-up at 3 months was among individuals who listed two or fewer informants. David et al. (2012) observed four or five "collaterals" as being a critical point in retaining participants over time following their release from prison.

Tracking adolescent study participants may be facilitated by including a variety of informants, beyond traditional nuclear and extended family information. For example, useful locator data might include social contacts in the peer group: including girlfriends/boyfriends, best friends, workplaces, and "hangouts" (street corners, malls, arcades, skateboard parks, hair/nail salons). School-based contacts (teachers, coaches, guidance counselors) may be possible if proper documentation and release of information forms are secured in compliance with local standards and the federal Family Educational Rights and Privacy Act (FERPA). As a cautionary note, one study team reported strong retention rates (85%–91%) in work with adolescents assessed as having a substance use disorder when they conserved study resources and used only familial key informants; the study authors indicated that the adolescent participants did not favor study staff contacting people outside of their family members (Yetarian, Dow, & Kelly, 2012). Clearly, the take-home message concerns knowing your study participants and what works (or does not) for them.

The four-phase EVMC protocol is a tracking plan with demonstrated effectiveness in multiple studies involving adults who engage in substance misuse, as well as one study involving adolescents. EVMC stands for Engagement, Verification, Maintenance, and Confirmation (Scott, 2004; Yetarian, 2012). Engagement activities mean collecting contact information for participants and collateral informants, and scheduling the next interview session. Verification occurs shortly thereafter; the pieces of information are checked for accuracy and viability early enough that the participant is likely to be easily reached if there exist errors needing to be corrected. Maintenance activities are directed toward keeping participants engaged and include reconfirming addresses, thereby providing an alert system for changes that might be more easily resolved early rather than later. Confirmation is about making direct contact to remind and reconfirm appointments at a few points before the next scheduled data collection event. The tracking team's efforts at each of these stages are also monitored on a regular basis. This process is to be followed and repeated at each point of contact with participants.

Participant-Generated Letters

As an adjunct to identifying key informants in our prisoner reentry studies, each participant addressed a "Dear Informant" form letter to each of their listed key informants. Preceding any informant telephone calls from the project staff, these letters were sent to the key informants on behalf of participants. These letters reassured their key informants that the participant wished to be located by the project team, and gave the informant a chance to consult with the participant about informing

Box 3.1 "Dear Informant" Letter

College of Social Work

Stillman Hall
1947 N College Road
Columbus, OH 43210-1162

Phone (614) 292-6288
Fax (614) 292-6940
http://www.csw-ohio-state.edu

Dear _____,

I have given the following people permission to contact you to help locate me for an interview on Project RISE. Please help them get in touch with me.

☐ Dr. Audrey Begun
☐ (project coordinator name)
☐ (research assistant name)
☐ (research assistant name)

Signed,

_____

(signature)

_____

(printed name)

_____

(date)

project staff, as well. The letters were written generically so that participant involvement in the study was nonstigmatizing. Participants personalized the "Dear _____" and "signed by" sections, in their own handwriting, with the names/nickname that they use for each other: "Dear Mom," "Dear Gram," "Dear BB" and signed "Your Niece, Shel" or "Your Daughter, Min" (see Box 3.1).

Telephone, Mail, and Text Messaging

In addition to updating tracking information during each study appointment, contacts between intervention and data collection sessions might include a combination of telephone or text "check-in" contacts and appointment reminders, mailing seasonal greeting cards, and delivering appointment reminders. The use of text messaging has gained recent momentum in participant retention in intervention research. This is due, in part, to its ease of use, low cost, and in some cases, preference on the part of participants—especially among younger adults (Hightower, n.d.; Materia et al., 2016). For example, text messaging can be used to send appointment reminders or to prompt participants to complete journal entries or online assessments. Secure survey links can be embedded in text messages, thereby promoting participant retention in ongoing data collection activities. Some investigators also have found that text messaging has been helpful in reaching participants who may not be as responsive to other more established communication channels, such as e-mail and phone (Hightower, n.d.).

At this time, it appears that text messaging in intervention research is useful as a research facilitation tool rather than as a data collection tool, especially if a study is subject to the Health Insurance Portability and Accountability Act (HIPAA). While it has earned some degree of popularity in survey research, text messaging like any communication technology is not 100% secured (Greene, 2012). The biggest concern with e-mail and text messaging of data in intervention studies is the potential breach of participant confidentiality (Greene, 2012). Although messages may be encrypted, a breach of confidentiality with clinical data has the potential to exceed minimal risk to the participant. The potential loss or theft of a study team's smartphone is a source of concern with text messages; a password-protected phone may help to minimize this risk. In the consent process, the study team might wish to inform participants about how to password-protect their own phones to improve confidentiality protection, as well. A permanent text deletion plan, particularly for e-mail data, also is needed for study messages at the conclusion of data management, since a third-party server company (e.g., Google or Yahoo) may retain a copy of the information exchanged (Greene, 2012). Finally, staff training about best practices for the use of text messaging in intervention research also will help to minimize risks to participant confidentiality (Green, 2012).

Locator Services

Because behavioral health research often involves populations that lack residential stability, investigators may wish to develop tracking protocols that incorporate the use of public and/or commercial locator databases or commercial credit agencies should they become lost to follow-up. Cotter et al. (2002) provide a list of helpful websites and public access databases useful for locating participants; others may have emerged since their article was published. They provide wise advice about carefully investigating any site or service before entering into a contractual agreement. There are important privacy issues that need to be addressed in the IRB protocol and participant consent procedures, since some of these sites have "small print" rules that allow them to use your search information in ways that potentially intrude on participants' privacy.

Reducing Participant Burden

Investigators who incur significant cost and extend considerable effort toward recruiting study participants, particularly difficult-to-access populations, often find themselves greatly tempted to collect as much data as could ever conceivably be of interest. An unfortunate consequence is the effect on study retention stemming from the increased participant burden. Also, the less relevant the data collection is to the reasons why participants originally volunteered, the more likely participants may be to drop out of the research activities. Overly zealous assessment batteries may, therefore, interfere with the central study aim of determining feasibility, efficacy, or effectiveness of an intervention. It is advisable to carefully review and possibly censor the assessment procedures and data collection tools for participant burden, relevance, and interest value (Hinshaw et al., 2004). Additional research measures may need to be saved for future research studies. Including flexible choices in the format of data collection tools (e.g., written, oral, audio-assisted computer administration) can also enhance retention among participants (Armistead et al., 2004). However, use of technology in data collection may also tempt investigators to add measures that increase participant burden, thus requiring a thoughtful approach to the inclusion of technology-enhanced data collection strategies.

To gauge participant burden, pilot test the entire research protocol with representatives from the participant populations (Keller, Gonzales, & Fleuriet, 2005). For example, in studying the intersection of substance use, sexual risk, and trauma history among women living in urban housing developments, our initial study protocol involved two separate baseline assessments within a 1-week period. However, when given the option, most participants preferred a single, longer appointment, rather than coming for two separate appointments; ironically, the purpose of separating these assessment appointments was to reduce participant burden! Study retention rates increased with offering this IRB-approved longer, single session option (and providing a meal).

Incentive Payments

As noted in chapter 2 about participant recruitment, delivering incentive payments to study participants has a long tradition in behavioral intervention studies. The presentation of the incentive as a payment in appreciation of a person's time and efforts may be more likely to promote retention than portraying incentives as a "gift" or "favor" to the participant (Taylor, 2009). Taylor (2009) also recommends paying the interview incentive at the beginning of a session, rather than the end, as a means of communicating the value and importance of the participant's contributions, and as an element of the social exchange process and trust-building.

The issue of participant incentive payments is not without controversy, despite being a common practice in health and behavioral health research. Festinger et al. (2005) analyzed two potential ethical concerns associated with paying participants engaged in research studies: the potential for participant coercion or encouraging participants to engage in unhealthy behaviors (e.g., substance misuse). Investigators must address with their IRBs the degree to which the amount or type of incentive may be coercive: encouraging individuals to participate in research that is not in their own interests simply to gain the incentive. Festinger's team (2005) randomly assigned study participants to one of six different incentive conditions; $10, $40, or $70 in either cash or gift card form. They concluded that incentive conditions were unrelated to participants' new substance use, sense of coercion to participate, or purposes for which the incentive monies were reportedly used. Amount and type of payment did, however, relate to participants' level of satisfaction with study involvement (larger cash payments being most effective), and larger amounts in either form were associated with greater ease of tracking for the follow-up interviews. It is not clear how these data might need to be adjusted for the current economy, or if distinctions between cash and gift cards might be different in the current marketplace.

As a means of enhancing participant retention in study activities, it is crucial to consider these issues in balance with the amounts and forms of incentive payment that participants find meaningful. In a survey of researchers directing National Institute on Drug Abuse–funded projects, the authors observed that interview protocols for data collection were compensated at rates two to three times higher than for the collection of biological samples (Farabee, Hawken, & Griffith, 2011). Furthermore, they observed a significant relationship between the rate of compensation and success in collecting longitudinal follow-up data: studies achieving 80% follow-up or greater provided significantly higher incentive payments than did studies reporting lower than 80% rates.

If working with new or unfamiliar populations, we strongly urge investigators to conduct preliminary focus groups to ascertain the "tipping point" in amounts and types of incentives. For example, while gift cards to local merchants appear to be meaningful in many communities, it is important to determine which specific merchants. In one study of women leaving jail, participants selected cards to Vendor A almost exclusively over Vendor B; in another community, men and women leaving jails and prisons almost exclusively selected the Vendor B gift cards over Vendor A. None of the participants in our recent studies wanted to receive university issued checks, as they had no means of cashing them without paying check cashing fees to do so. Farabee et al. (2016) reported on a randomized, longitudinal trial using rechargeable incentive cards or money orders as incentive payments for maintaining their contact information in the study tracking system. Individuals with a substance use history were more responsive to the "immediate gratification" rechargeable cards than to the money orders delivered by mail. Without more studies of this type to rely on, we urge the use of focus groups to inform the selection of incentive types and amounts. Payment in forms other than checks may require careful negotiation and documentation for auditing purposes at the researchers' home institutions, and the audit trail may need to be negotiated with IRBs to protect confidentiality.

A set of concerns also worthy of exploration, possibly through focus groups, involves how to safely and reliably deliver incentive payments.

We do not want to make participants vulnerable to exploitation or violence as a result of receiving an incentive payment. Nor do we want research staff to be vulnerable as a result of participants or others in the neighborhood knowing that incentives are being carried or stored on the premises. Furthermore, participants may not want to receive payments by mail because there is little assurance that they actually would be the final recipients. One incentive method used with success in our study of women in subsidized housing developments was use of gift cards that require activation by research staff after they are received by participants.

Yet another consideration for studies designed with repeated data collection episodes is to make multiple incentive payments and consider the option of gradually increasing the incentive level for maintaining participation over time. For example, completing the initial screening, intake, and randomization phases might involve one incentive payment; completing the next 3 months might involve a second, slightly higher incentive payment, and completing the final 3 months might involve a third, still higher payment level. We have employed this graduated or "stepped" incentive strategy with good success in studies of over a year in duration.

Participant Costs

In some cases, budgeting for incentive payments might also take into account incidental costs of participation (for example, see VanderWalde & Kurzban, 2011). Worth considering are public transportation or personal mileage and parking for participant travel to intervention or data collection sites, child care during intervention or data collection episodes, and snack foods, beverages, or meals during lengthy appointments. Covering study-related expenses is not an incentive payment.

What "works" in this arena may differ markedly by participant age, gender, family status, income level, ethnicity, neighborhood/community, and other characteristics of those engaged in a particular study. Issues around incentivizing participation would be useful to explore through focus group sessions with potential participants prior to committing resources to the incentive program; cultural relevance of certain types of incentives to relationship building, such as foods served during study sessions, should be explored (Keller, Gonzales, & Fleuriet,

2005). These cost reimbursements are factored into the IRB proposal and consent form.

Retention Techniques, Past and Present

Some retention recommendations presented in earlier literature are no longer feasible in this day and age. For example, many of the tracking approaches recommended by Cottler et al. (1996) require transfer of information from agencies no longer empowered to do so (e.g., Social Security Administration, public and private social service agencies, hospitals and treatment programs). Similarly, recommendations from Ribisl et al. (1996) regarding participant tracking through the use of informal relationships with other behavioral health service providers may be obsolete since enactment of HIPAA and the Federal Educational Rights and Privacy Act (FERPA).

Wipke-Tevis and Pickett (2008) discuss ways in which HIPAA policies have directly affected the recruitment and retention of intervention study participants. In addition to having less ease of access to participant data, increased complexity of the consent process, and increased administrative burdens, HIPAA impedes the use of strategies such as telephone and text messages, as well as mailed reminders with return addresses in which a person's diagnosis might be inferred.

Methods successfully used to enhance retention include multiple, different forms of communication with study participants. For example, in their work with college students, Berry and Bass (2012) offered mail, telephone, text messaging, Facebook, webpage, and e-mail options to their participants—contact information for all these formats appeared on their recruitment and retention materials. Furthermore, their participant registration materials allowed individuals to include any or all of these types of contact information about themselves and to prioritize the order in which they wished to have these sources used for communicating with them, thereby creating an individualized plan. Contents of these multiple forms of communication all should be IRB-approved, with both method and timing of delivery based on participant preference, which may vary depending on characteristics of the participant population. Technology and social media options such as e-mail reminders and text messages may come into question with regard to security and protection of personal information.

Participant Satisfaction

A final strategy to consider involves the use of instruments and procedures to assess participant satisfaction, in much the same way that programs measure client satisfaction. One benefit is that being asked about their experiences in the study can enhance participants' sense of connectedness and importance to the study (Verheggen, Nieman, Reerink, & Kok, 1998). The use of this strategy also can help study teams concerned with quality improvement to identify aspects of the intervention or study protocol that may contribute to participant attrition, as well as factors extrinsic to the protocols that may be affecting participant retention.

Participant satisfaction may be assessed using qualitative methods (see Verheggen, Nieman, Reerink, & Kok, 1998) or adapting quantitative client satisfaction tools to this purpose. Examples include the Client Satisfaction Inventory, available in English and Spanish versions (McMurtry & Hudson, 2000; McMurtry & Torres, 2002), and the Client Satisfaction Questionnaire in various forms and versions (Attkisson & Zwick, 1982; Larsen, Attkisson, Hargreaves, & Nguyen, 1979; Nguyen, Attkisson, & Stegner, 1984). One published tool assesses the satisfaction of healthy volunteers in clinical trials designed to test medications, and may be helpful in social work or behavioral health intervention studies (see Sramek et al., 2015). This 16-item survey addresses five aspects of the research experience, each item being rated on a 7-point scale of agreement. The five aspects are informed consent, participation, facilities, other experiences with clinical trials, and overall impression/future participation. In the public domain, the Substance Abuse and Mental Health Services Administration offers a patient satisfaction measurement tool, as well (http://www.integration.samhsa.gov/Patient_Satisfaction_Survey_-_English.pdf).

Adaptability

Developing flexible, adaptive menus of retention strategies may be the most cost-efficient approach in behavioral intervention research. For example, when conducting research in schools where high student absenteeism is an issue, be prepared to collect data on multiple occasions and to use alternative collection strategies, such as telephone interviews, home interviews, or mailed questionnaires, to maximize retention (Boys et al., 2003).

Cottler et al. (1996) describe a three-stage tracking strategy used in their study of HIV risk among individuals outside of the treatment system who are using substances: stage 1, telephone contacts; stage 2, tracking through systems (e.g., city/county coroner's offices, city and county warrant offices, city/county/state licensing and other records, federal, state and local probation and parole); and, stage 3, field operations involving family members and friends/neighbors, neighborhood hangouts, churches, social clubs, workplace(s), temporary employment agencies, and homeless shelters. These approaches are staged in terms of increasing commitment of resources.

Initially collecting information about identifying behaviors, language/accent, nickname, or other unique traits and physical marks (tattoos, piercings, unusual habits) may facilitate field-based tracking efforts (e.g., see Meyers, Webb, Frantz, & Randall, 2002). Ensuring adequate time and travel resources for engaging in the fieldwork are included in the recommendations offered by Desmond et al. (1995). In developing an adaptive menu, plan to use the simplest and cheapest tracking methods first, saving the more expensive strategies for more difficult cases (Ribisl et al., 1996). Investigators must ensure that permission to employ any or all of these strategies has been approved by the IRB and consent/assent to use them was acquired from each participant, as well.

Effort

Often in clinical practice settings, policy establishes limits on the number of missed appointments that are tolerated before a client is terminated or charged for missed appointments. There may be a temptation to utilize these same limits with intervention research. While it may be a good indicator of an intervention's real-world feasibility to follow agency policy on missed appointments, it is important to recall the distinction between study sessions for the purpose of delivering an intervention and sessions for the purpose of data collection. More generous, lenient criteria may be needed for participant retention in research activities; limiting the effort may result in significant participant loss and selective attrition.

Consider, for example, the analysis conducted by Cotter, Burke, Stouthamer-Loeber, and Loeber (2005), where the mean number of contacts required to complete interviews with a cohort of youth experiencing behavioral disorders was 5.81 attempts, and 10% of the group required over 21 attempts. In a 6-month follow-up study of adolescents engaged in substance abuse, half did not respond to basic telephone efforts, and 40% required six or more contacts for interview completion (Meyers, Webb, Frantz, & Randall, 2002). Scott (2004) reported on retention rates across several studies involving individuals engaged in substance abuse behavior: for two of the studies, 70% of the participants were retained with fewer than 23 contact attempts, while 33 and 38 contacts were necessary to achieve 90% retention. Between 10 and 35 contact attempts were required to collect follow-up data from 21% of participants in a study of adults receiving a drug treatment protocol, and the greatest difficulty was with incarcerated individuals (Nemes et al., 2002). And, study participants provided with residential treatment following DUI charges (driving under the influence of alcohol or other substances) required an average 8.6 telephone calls (median 5.0) to collect 1-year follow-up data, and there continued to be a benefit between 10 and 40 call attempts, after which additional effort was deemed unjustified by the outcome (Kleschinsky et al., 2009).

Tracking and recontact effort can be highly skewed, with maximum effort required for a subgroup of a study sample (Walton et al., 1998). For example, following participants in a study addressing experiences of intimate partner violence, Clough et al. (2011) delineated the amount of effort budgeted for tracking and midpoint contact activities: quarterly contacts over 18 months were estimated at 24 hours per participant, plus 6 hours in documentation, time for a total of 30 hours each. Their "intensive effort group" required over 17 attempts to complete (compared to the "minimal effort group" requiring 4 attempts). Similarly, in their 18-month follow-up study, Cottler et al. (1996) reported an average of 22.5 attempts at locating their most-difficult-to-retain participants (13.6% were reached outside of the 70-day study window), compared to an average 5.4 attempts for the 86.4% who were more easily retained (reached within the 70-day study window). In the case of one community reentry study involving recently released prison and jail inmates, we determined that six missed data collection appointments was the optimal limit for terminating effort: almost 20% of participant data were collected in the fourth through sixth scheduled appointments.

Monitoring retention throughout the course of a study, and providing more detailed reporting in the research literature, may assist investigators in determining the optimal "tipping point" for these efforts where there begin to be diminishing returns in study retention (for example, see David, Alati, Ware, & Kinner, 2013). Planning ahead for encountering a "difficult to reach" subsample needing a diverse range in strategies and level of effort is also advised (Kleschinsky et al., 2009; Meyers, Webb, Frantz, & Randall, 2002). For example, Navratil et al. (1994) identified four categories of study participants and the retention strategies most appropriate for each:

- the "difficult to schedule" participants responded to persistence, empathy, and flexibility;
- "reluctant to continue" participants required attention to the relationship and rapport with the study;
- the "refusing" participant (usually the child in their study) was best recontacted later with personalized correspondence that emphasized the importance of their contributions to the research, assuming that the initial refusal was circumstantial or situational (given that the boys were in the study because of "disruptive behavioral disorders"); and,
- "transient" participants were tracked down through persistence.

The point concerning effort is eloquently made by the statement: "The importance of allocating adequate time for locating participants cannot be overstated" (Clough et al., 2011, p. 93). Cottler et al. (1996) also asserted that persistence is the key to successful study retention. Allocating sufficient budget resources is also critical. For example, Meyers et al. (2002) reported spending an estimated average of $85 more per participant than they had originally budgeted, per follow-up wave, to adequately track, locate, and interview adolescent research participants.

An equally important point to consider is this: at what point does "persistent effort" become participant harassment? Institutional review boards may raise these concerns, but even if they do not, the investigators need to establish a protocol for recognizing when enough is enough for any specific participant—what might be the participant's signals and clearly communicated options for a participant to request that retention efforts be stopped. It may also be helpful to discuss with participants up front what resources will be devoted to tracking and locating, so that there is a common understanding of the efforts that may be undertaken by the study to maintain their participation. At the other end, there may be some benefit gained in conveying a "last chance" message to participants. In other words, it is made clear that no future requests or attempts to contact them will be made, and they have this one last opportunity for their participation to make a difference in the project. Finally, if it is possible to do so considering the IRB-approved study protocol, leaving the option open for participants to contact study staff should they change their minds about study participation may facilitate data collection at more distal follow-up points, even when those participants seemed "lost" to follow-up.

Responding to Dynamic Situations

In designing a behavioral intervention study it is worthwhile to consider how to retain participants whose eligibility or availability for the study may fluctuate over time. For example, a person's condition may worsen or improve over the course of a study. If study protocols impose static, categorical criteria for inclusion and exclusion, study attrition is likely to be higher than if study protocols take into account fluctuations over time (e.g., a person's diagnostic status changes; demographic characteristics change; relationship or residency status changes; behaviors are inconsistent, such as failing to abstain from substance use, relapsing into violence toward a family member; another outside-of-study treatment modality is added).

Dynamic circumstances form a particularly challenging aspect of longitudinal intervention research involving populations. For example, there are many different ways in which participants involved with the criminal justice system become unavailable or ineligible due to sanctions imposed by the system rather than for reasons related to motivation for remaining in the study (e.g., rearrest for outstanding rather than new charges, being moved between facilities for administrative rather than behavioral reasons, being moved from one unit or program to another). Another dynamic feature that often arises with intervention research is the tendency for participants to engage in additional/supplemental interventions which may render them no longer eligible for study inclusion. Bell et al. (2008) suggested that competition between different intervention studies may be a contributing factor to study attrition, as individuals may explore and engage options that preclude their being maintained in a controlled study protocol.

In designing study inclusion and exclusion criteria, it is useful to take into consideration the fact that study participants are busy living their lives outside of their time in the study: when their life circumstances change, so might their availability to participate in the study. The more easily study protocols respond to circumstances such as changes in employment, residential, marital, child-care, and other factors, the less likely these factors will present significant barriers to participant retention. One study of preadolescent boys with "disruptive behavior disorders" reporting high retention rates at 4-years follow-up had 54% of the data collected outside of typical office hours, on evenings and weekends (Navratil et al., 1994). Additional elements for consideration include offering makeup sessions, allowing for alternative data collection methods (e.g., telephone interviews), incorporating flexible time windows for data collection contacts, and identifying which data points can be missed if absolutely necessary. For example, intervention investigators could at least ensure the collection of endpoint/outcome data (see The COMBINE Study Research Group, 2003). Furthermore, postattrition "exit interviews" may be conducted with those who drop out of the study in order to facilitate the development of retention-problem solutions.

A final point related to monitoring participant retention patterns is worth explaining. We have encountered novice investigators who initially are confused by this recommendation because they have learned that it is unwise to analyze data before a study is complete. The confusion clears when they understand the distinction between retention information and the data collected for the purposes of testing study hypotheses. Monitoring of the retention pattern data is distinctly different and crucially important to ensuring the quality of the intervention data to be analyzed at the study's conclusion.

CHAPTER SUMMARY

The literature offers insights into the impact of retention failure on intervention study results; combined with our experiences, literature offers insights concerning how retention might be managed and improved in behavioral intervention studies. Clearly, participant retention is a critical aspect of design and implementation in behavioral intervention investigations. Of paramount importance is regular monitoring of retention and attrition patterns throughout the course of a study. In planning intervention studies, investigators need to develop tailored retention processes, applying more flexible menus of retention options. The challenge lies in creating tailored approaches that facilitate retention without creating methodological variance that introduces systematic error and confounds study results.

In addition, there exists a niche in social and behavioral research for the study of retention methodologies and their relative cost-effectiveness. Investigators are encouraged to engage in dissemination activities whereby retention and attrition evidence may be shared across the research community, including analyses comparing strategies and the characteristics of participants retained with greater versus lesser degrees of difficulty. As this type of methodology information falls victim to increasing pressure for word/page limits to manuscripts, investigators and disciplines should develop new mechanisms for its dissemination. For example, we might post brief reports on our research or institutional websites, or develop electronic repositories whereby this information can be easily searched and located by other investigators. Finally, research can contribute to better understanding of the costs involved with strong retention plans; knowledge critical to helping investigators budget dollars, time, travel resources, and skilled/motivated staff for retention activities.

4

Planning Tools for Participant Recruitment and Retention

In the previous three chapters we explored the importance of developing adequate recruitment and retention plans, and we identified various strategies for how participant recruitment and retention plans might effectively be implemented. In this chapter, we identify specific planning skills and introduce tools to help investigators fine-tune their participant recruitment and retention plans. Four major areas of emphasis in this chapter[1] are: (1) setting recruitment and retention goals, (2) steps in the process, (3) budgeting for participant recruitment and retention, and (4) cost-effectiveness of recruitment strategies.

A basic premise underlying the contents of this chapter is that investigators need to allocate sufficient funds, time, effort, staff, and other resources to ensure successful participant recruitment and retention to meet their study goals and objectives. Another basic premise is that

---

[1] Portions of this chapter are reprinted, with permission, from Berger, Begun, and Otto-Salaj (2009).

investigators need to be realistic about the recruitment and retention goals that they establish for their studies. As discussed in chapters 2 and 3, a potentially disastrous yet relatively common error involves investigators being overly ambitious about their ability to recruit and subsequently retain study participants. The consequences obviously may lead to study failure. Additionally, consider that reviewers of grant proposals, based on their own experiences, often have a sense of what is feasible in terms of recruitment and retention, and either rate grant proposals or advise funding agencies accordingly. Consider, too, the complications involved with repeatedly submitting protocol amendments to an institutional review board (IRB) to cover additional recruitment and retention efforts, the need for which was not initially envisioned.

SETTING PARTICIPANT RECRUITMENT AND RETENTION GOALS

"How many participants do I need to recruit into my study?" is a common question with multiple types of answers. There are several steps involved in answering this study design question. What is crucial to remember is that the numbers indicate how many participants we need for conducting our planned statistical analyses, not how many we need to initially recruit! Thus, we begin at the end, and work our way back from those terminal numbers toward our initial recruitment goals. In other words, accuracy in determining how many participants we need to recruit starts with knowing how many we need at the point of data analysis combined with estimates of how many we believe we will be able to retain or estimates of our attrition rate.

Beginning at the End

There are many resources available to help an investigator determine the needed sample size for a study. One set of decisions that must be made at the outset involves the nature of statistical analyses that will be performed, determined by the study questions, measurement tools, nature of the variables included, and the sampling strategies to be employed. For example, if we are planning to compare two different intervention groups on a single, normally distributed outcome variable, and our study participants were randomly selected from the population, we might consider the example of one-way analysis of variance (ANOVA). The answer to our "How many do I need?" question might be derived from a traditional rule of thumb: 7–10 participants per study design cell as a minimum.

Fortunately or unfortunately, data analytic plans often are far more complex these days, yet often more forgiving in terms of underlying assumptions than in the past. As we increasingly engage in regression-based analytic approaches that deal with hierarchically nested data, latent variables, data with multiple measurement points, subgroup comparisons, and mediator or moderator variables, old rules of thumb no longer serve us well. Furthermore, in intervention science, it is no longer sufficient to demonstrate a statistically significant difference between treatment groups, we are also concerned with clinical significance and effect sizes of the observed differences.

All of this makes it more complicated to answer our initial question about how many study participants are needed. For this, we will need to consider factors such as statistical power, effect size, stratified sampling to fill study design "cells," attrition patterns, and intention-to-treat designs.

Statistical Power

Statistical power is a principle that has an important relationship to sample size. Statistical power is concerned with the ability to accurately detect a significant difference between two intervention conditions (or other research design components) when a true difference exists—thus, circumventing the Type II error (failing to reject the null hypothesis of no difference when a difference actually exists; revisit Figure 1.4). A convention in social and behavioral research is to accept a Type II error probability of .20, meaning that we are willing to accept a 20% chance of being wrong in this way (see Sullivan & Feinn, 2012). This translates into a power coefficient of .80 (an 80% chance of being correct), calculated as the ideal 100% chance of being correct minus the 20% acceptable chance of being wrong. In other words, applying the .20 Type II error convention, we would be aiming for a power level of .80.

Power analysis is an approach to mathematically calculate an estimate for the number of participants needed to complete a particular study. To generate the estimate, additional decisions need to be made and pieces of information secured. Two of these concern the effect size of the intervention (or comparison) being tested and the criterion level for alpha (α) applied in testing the comparison hypotheses. Once the criterion level for the alpha (α) and an effect size of the intervention being tested are known, the necessary sample size can be computed depending on the type of statistical analyses planned for the intervention outcome data.

Alpha Criterion Level

The first task is to identify a desired alpha criterion point. Traditionally, in behavioral research, the value of $\alpha = .05$ is adopted as the criterion point below which a calculated p-value leads to rejection of the null hypothesis. In other words, with $p < .05$ (in a two-tailed statistical test) we believe that it is safe to reject the hypothesis of no difference existing between the conditions being compared. In terms of confidence intervals, if $\alpha = .05$, then we are interested in confidence levels of .95 (or, $1 - \alpha$). When the value "0" (no difference) lies outside of our .95 confidence interval, then we are comfortable rejecting the null hypothesis.

Effect Size

The next task is to estimate the target effect size. Effect size is an estimate of the magnitude of an observed difference between groups. We might find a statistically significant difference on an outcome variable between an intervention and treatment as usual (TAU) control group. This does not tell us all that we want to know, however, about that observed difference (see Sullivan & Feinn, 2012). For example, if intelligence quotient (IQ) is our outcome measure of interest, what if the average difference were one or two IQ points? Would we care to invest much in that intervention for such a small average gain, a gain that is clinically not very meaningful? On the other hand, what if the average difference were 20 IQ points? We might be quite interested! The size of our sample influences the significance level (p being less than our $\alpha = .05$ criterion point): Even if the magnitude of the impact from our intervention is not impressive, large sample sizes alone might contribute to statistical significance. We aim simultaneously for both strong power and large effect sizes in intervention research.

Knowing about the effect size can help us properly interpret statistical results for our intervention study. This point is demonstrated in the example from correlational data in a study of readiness to change intimate partner violence behavior conducted with 500 men at entry to a mandated batterer treatment program. The correlation we observed between a person's past number of violent intimate partner relationships and present readiness to change intimate partner behavior was statistically significant at the $p < .01$ level; the greater the number of violent relationships they reported, the higher were their readiness scores. However, the magnitude of this correlation was small: only 0.14, which on a scale from –1.0 to +1.0 is pretty close to zero. In other words, the size of the effect was nothing to write home about, even though it was statistically significant. The large number of study participants contributed to statistical significance.

On the other hand, using the same data set, we can look at the participants' readiness to change scores between intake to and completion of a treatment program. A paired t-test comparing readiness scores at the two time points was statistically significant. The mean readiness score at program completion was higher than the mean at program intake: $M_{post} = 5.28$, $M_{pre} = 4.57$, $t(185) = -7.99$, $p < .001$. How powerful was the effect? Correcting for the paired nature of the pre/post data (the correlation coefficient was 0.533), a within-subjects effect size was computed: Cohen's $d = 0.587$ (see effect size calculator by Lee Becker at University of Colorado–Colorado Springs, www.uccs.edu/lbecker). According to the tradition originally established by Cohen, an effect size of 0.2 is considered small, 0.5 medium, and 0.8 or higher is large (see following discussion for more detail). Thus, the relationship was statistically significant, in the desired direction, and of a medium magnitude effect size.

This example reflects effect sizes in a completed study where other parameters are known. Where does effect size come into play when proposing an intervention study and the outcomes are not yet known? One suggestion appearing in the literature is to conduct pilot studies of your interventions in order to determine a reasonable effect size (e.g., Sullivan & Feinn, 2012). Others have argued that this is not a sufficient reason to conduct a pilot study (e.g., Kraemer, Mintz,

Noda, Tinklenberg, & Yesavage, 2006). Their point is basically that a small-sample pilot study is not going to be informative on this point because the standard error of the effect size is unreasonably large; as a result, the pilot-study sample may need to be as large as the ultimate proposed study, which negates the usefulness of applying scarce resources to conducting the pilot study rather than just conducting the proposed study. They argue that there may be valid reasons for conducting pilot studies, but doing them simply in order to determine effect size is not one of them.

Instead, we might rely on two other approaches suggested by Sullivan and Feinn (2012). The first of these is to consult the existing literature about the planned intervention approach. For an innovative intervention, it may be possible to make "best guesses" based on similar interventions and resulting effect sizes found in studies examining them. However, because of the innovative nature of the intervention to be studied, these would still be guesses. Thus, it may be preferable to turn to the second of the alternatives: determine what would be a minimal meaningful, sufficiently important clinical difference to observe. For example, Miller and Manuel (2008) conducted a survey of practicing addiction treatment professionals to determine "how large of a difference matters" before these professionals would be interested in learning to deliver the new treatment (p. 525). The meaningful differences represented the percent of clients who were "doing well" with the treatment approaches being compared. The practitioners identified about a 10%–12% difference on outcomes such as total abstinence and full-time, legal employment within 1 year following treatment between the two approaches as being clinically meaningful to them and warranting their learning to deliver the new approach. Among other meaningful differences were the number of days clients used substances. An intervention that halved this number was meaningful to the practitioners. Doubling the number of days abstinent was the other meaningful tipping point.

Miller and Manuel (2008) suggest that using practitioner-derived, clinically meaningful treatment effects could be used to power clinical trials for detecting outcome differences versus estimating an effect size (e.g., from previous literature) and then determining the sample size needed to achieve statistical significance of the effect. This could result in intervention studies with smaller sample sizes, which in turn would be less costly to conduct. Another convention in social and behavioral

Table 4.1   Effect Size Indices[a]

Statistical test	Effect size index	Small	Medium	Large
t-test of means	**d**	0.20	0.50	0.80
t-test of correlations	**r**	0.10	0.30	0.50
F-test ANOVA	**f**	0.10	0.25	0.40
F-test regression	**f²**	0.02	0.15	0.35
chi-square test	**w**	0.10	0.30	0.50

[a]Modified from psych.wisc.edu/henriques/power.html

research is to rely on the definitions of small, medium, and large effect size presented by Jacob Cohen (1988, 1992). The effect size coefficients associated with these three levels differ in terms of the type of statistical test involved (see Table 4.1).

Sample Size Computation

Cohen (1992) presents a table of minimal sample sizes necessary for small, medium, and large effect sizes (ES), given the specific power level of .80, at three different α levels, for different types of statistical tests. Here we present a modified version of that table (see Table 4.2) for just $\alpha = .05$. From the table you can see that we will need to plan for larger sized samples when we want to be able to detect more subtle, minute effect sizes; smaller sample sizes will limit us to only being able to detect larger effects. One way to think about this is in terms of magnification power: We need a stronger, more powerful microscope lens in order to see the smaller, finer aspects of what we are studying, whereas a less powerful lens may suffice in seeing the larger, gross aspects.

In addition to the figures presented in Table 4.2, consider that Cohen computed a need for larger sample sizes with an α level smaller than our .05 convention. For example, with an ANOVA comparing two treatment groups we needed 64 participants per group to detect a medium effect size when we adopted a criterion point of $\alpha = .05$. However, if we wanted to be more conservative on our risk of a Type I error (rejecting the null hypothesis when we should not have done so), and adopted an $\alpha = .01$ criterion point, we would need 95 participants per group.

Calculating the necessary sample size is also dependent on the nature of the statistical analyses planned for the outcome data. The list

Table 4.2 Cohen's Estimated Sample Size for Three Effect Sizes, Power = .80, α = .05

Statistical Test	Small	Medium	Large
t-test for two independent means	393 per group	64 per group	26 per group
chi-square test for goodness of fit (depends on degrees of freedom, df)			
1 df	785 total sample	87 total sample	26 total sample
2 df	964 total sample	107 total sample	39 total sample
3 df	1,090 total sample	121 total sample	44 total sample
4 df	1,194 total sample	133 total sample	48 total sample
one-way ANOVA assuming equal variances (depends on number of groups compared)			
2 groups	393 per group	64 per group	26 per group
3 groups	322 per group	52 per group	21 per group
4 groups	274 per group	45 per group	18 per group

of statistical approaches presented in Cohen's recommendations may not suffice for your planned intervention study. Here is an example used in planning a study to compare an enhanced brief intervention for facilitating treatment engagement by patients with a substance use disorder with a standard brief intervention. In this case, previous research suggested that effect sizes between 0.31 and 0.56 may be reasonably expected (Burke, Arkowitz, & Menchola, 2003; Saitz et al., 2009). Therefore, we opted to use the more conservative lower value (which would require a larger sample size). The analysis plan included group comparisons, two-tailed significance tests, an α = .05, four time points, and average change over time. Applying a 20% anticipated attrition rate for the total sample was adopted as it reflects a standard practice in intervention research on substance misuse. Based on this information, about 113 eligible patients were deemed needed in each group at the start of the study to research a power level of 0.80 for analyses at the end.

Several freely accessible interactive websites allow an investigator to easily compute minimum sample size. For example, G*Power allows computation for a number of different statistical approaches, and is free to download (http://www.gpower.hhu.de/); recent versions of statistical packages already in use by an investigator, such as R and Stata include the ability to compute necessary sample size, and other "add on" packages can be purchased for this purpose, as well (e.g., IBM's SPSS SamplePower or PROC POWER in PPS for SAS). Unfortunately, many of these tools are designed to assist survey researchers concerned with response margin of error, not intervention or evaluation researchers comparing groups. Nor are all of them responsive to the repeated measures design associated with longitudinal studies.

Important to remember is that the minimum sample sizes calculated with these tools generally are the number needed at the point of final analysis, based on your study design. You still need to calculate the number needed to recruit based on your anticipated rates of attrition from the study, as well as other reasons for data loss (e.g., incomplete or missing data). Finally, investigators should also consider what the maximum sample size will be. Since each participant engaged in a study "costs" precious resources, it is helpful to know where the cutoff point will be. Furthermore, this figure is required by many IRBs, as it is an indication of how many individuals will be shouldering the burden of study participation and assuming the potential risks. For these reasons, the maximum figure desired should be reasonably close to the minimum required. While we have presented an overview of the process of determining sample size here, a resource to consult for greater depth and breadth of the topic's coverage is Dattalo's (2008) book that explains how investigators might balance the issues of statistical power, precision, and practical concerns such as study costs.

Stratified Samples

The overall study design is an important overlay to consider when calculating the "needed numbers" for your study. If a study aim involves exploring the role of certain demographic features (e.g., age, gender, diagnosis, race/ethnicity, economic status) as moderator variables, you will need to ensure sufficient representation in each of the relevant categories to satisfy the demands of the study design. For example, if we were designing a study to determine whether clients' low versus high readiness to change intimate partner violence behaviors (measured as a dichotomous variable at program intake) has an impact on how much behavior change is associated with contrasted treatment protocols, we would need to ensure not only sufficient numbers of participants at the end of the study to test the treatment but also sufficient numbers of individuals meeting criteria for the low as well as high readiness to change groups.

This raises the issue of nonrandom attrition as a phenomenon around which planning may need to be done (see chapter 3). Considering the brief example just discussed, we might find that initial recruitment of equal numbers of participants into the low and high readiness to change groups proceeds as planned, however our retention over the course of the longitudinal intervention study does not. Imagine that our overall retention rate was 70% (meaning that we lost 30% through attrition along the way), but we did not randomly lose 30% from each group. Perhaps we lost considerably more from the group with low readiness compared to the other. With this systematic trend in attrition, our final study results are going to be biased and unreliable.

Multisite Studies

Even in large communities, individual investigators or study teams may find it difficult to recruit sufficient participant numbers, especially when the phenomenon under study is uncommon or stigmatized. Collaborative research partnerships offer one solution to the problem. Consider, for example, the National Institute on Drug Abuse (NIDA) Treatment Clinical Trials Network (CTN). Treatment clinical trials are conducted through 12 nodes and one consortium where study efforts are coordinated (see http://www.drugabuse.gov/about-nida/organiza-tion/cctn/ctn/about-ctn). As a result, behavioral and pharmacological intervention studies can be conducted at multiple, coordinated sites to increase not only the numbers of study participants but also their representativeness across regions of the country. Multisite studies often occur on a smaller scale as well, with investigator teams coordinating their efforts to simultaneously conduct a study in multiple locations. Each location alone might not be able to generate sufficient numbers and diversity of study participants due to an insufficiently "deep" participant pool, but in combination and with strong coordination they may be able achieve exceptional goals.

STEPS IN THE PLANNING PROCESS

Next, creating an adequate recruitment and retention budget is facilitated by having the ability to accurately identify the component activities and products required to accomplish the study goals. This section provides a list of possible elements to consider and discusses some of the nuances involved. These are listed under the following categories: identifying the target population, identifying recruitment options, developing and producing recruitment and retention materials, disseminating materials, developing tracking systems, responding and screening, consenting, enrolling, and retaining participants.

Identifying the Target Population

This task integrates much of the content from chapters 2 and 3, as well as the sample size content from earlier in this chapter. In essence, it is about specifying who the target population for the study might be, in such a way that it is clear who should be included in the sample representing that population. This also includes specifying the numbers needed overall, as well as the numbers of individuals of various types, groups, or subgroups expressing specific characteristics (i.e., demographic characteristics, diagnoses, problem severity, treatment condition to which they are assigned). Thus, this step includes identifying the specific inclusion/exclusion criteria to be applied, as well as the specific tools and procedures to be employed in the prescreening and screening processes—preferably, psychometrically sound instruments and procedures supported by evidence. Four strategies to consider for informing this step are:

- consulting the literature about the problem or population to which the intervention or program is directed,
- focus groups or other forms of consultation involving members of the target population,
- inclusion of members of the target population on the study team, and
- consultation with providers who are experienced with the population for whom the intervention or program was developed.

In addition to soliciting consultation, members of the project team may engage in liaison activities with agencies, programs, and service providers in the community. Distinct from consultation to gather advice about recruitment and retention, the purpose of these two-way conversations and relationship-building activities is to build a referral system by which they might refer potential participants to the intervention study, and back to which participants might be referred should they need services beyond the scope of the study or if an individual seeking intervention does not meet the study inclusion criteria.

This planning step may already have been completed in order to submit funding proposals for an intervention project. Prior to study implementation, however, these plans need to be revisited and potentially modified. The time spent in review and modification might need to be included in budgeting staff time and effort.

Identifying Direct and Indirect Recruitment Options

The list of options for a project team to consider related to direct participant recruitment (with implications for retention) includes categories such as:

- mass media advertising (radio and television ads, billboards, movie theater ads),
- print media advertising (direct mailing, newspaper ads, newsletters and bulletins of programs/agencies/organizations),
- bus and bus-stop placards,
- presentations to community groups,
- posters, banners, flags, flyers, and information cards,
- study branding/logo and branded mailings and giveaways (pens, T-shirts, etc.),
- participant registries and pools,
- press releases and public service announcements,
- social media tools (Craigslist, Facebook, Twitter, LinkedIn, Tumblr, e-mail lists/ listservs), and
- incentive payments.

Indirect recruitment options are those directed at referral networks rather than directed to potential participants themselves. Some options for indirect recruitment pathways include:

- announcements to referral network/service providers, advertising with professional organizations,
- presentations to professional groups, including staff meetings and in-service trainings, and
- word-of-mouth, snowball, or respondent-driven sampling.

Several activities listed here need further explanation. First, providing tear-off strips at the bottom of a poster can be problematic—not only does it end up looking unkempt, the information that can be taken away on the strip is minimal and the number of strips that fit on a single poster is limited. One option is to apply a set of preprinted Post-it notes as the take-away. These can hold more information, do not affect the poster's appearance when removed, and larger numbers can be placed (and replaced) on a poster. A contemporary option is to print a QR (quick response) code on the poster. This permits individuals with portable technology (e.g., smartphone or tablet) to capture a link to the study website (URL) where contact can be made or to a video presentation with more information about the project. Finally, it may be preferable to place stacks of postcard-sized flyers in some locations rather than hanging posters. One word of caution about this: We had an instance where individuals took the flyers and attempted to use them as part of a fundraising scam, soliciting cash "donations" for the research project.

Also related to the use of posters and flyers is strategically planning where these will be placed to best reach your intended audiences. For example, if the research topic is somewhat personal or sensitive, you might want them in places where individuals can read them in relative privacy—patient treatment rooms, restroom stalls, or dressing rooms may be options, with proper management approval. Consider placing them where individuals will be waiting and perhaps picking up reading material, such as clinic waiting areas or treatment rooms; perhaps even car wash and repair facilities, or barber/beauty/nail/massage salons. It may be possible to arrange that flyers be distributed as part of naturally occurring distribution events, such as attached to pizza delivery boxes or other carryout orders in the neighborhood where you hope to recruit participants. You might make them available at community health fairs or other public events where service providers are welcome to advertise. These may or may not have associated fees. Each option will need to be approved by the IRB prior to employment, as well.

In regard to public service announcements, while these may be disseminated without charge, they must meet very specific criteria. Their purpose is to raise awareness of an issue, or to change public attitudes and behaviors. Thus, their focus is narrow, they provide a brief but pointed message, and they cannot use directive language. This means that instead of saying, "Call this number" the wording would be along the lines of, "This number can provide more information." Furthermore, your team will have little control over when these announcements are aired, so you may not have a good fit with when your target audience sees or hears them. Press releases also are disseminated without charge to your team and suffer from a similar loss of control over the message. While you may provide the media enterprise with a well-crafted release, it may be edited to suit the newspaper, radio, or television producers.

Respondent-Driven Sampling

Finally, because these topics are so well developed in many research textbooks and resources, we have not discussed general sampling techniques, such as "snowball" sampling (see, for example, those listed in chapter 1). We did, however, want to draw attention to respondent-driven sampling, because this approach may be unique in that it employs individuals other than study staff in the participant recruitment process. In brief, the method integrates social network analysis approaches with a participant-based, chain-referral system for generating new participant contacts. There are both advantages and challenges involved with this approach which is best applied in situations where stigma or other factors make it difficult for investigators to identify members of "hidden" populations but where these individuals may know about each other (see Heckathorn, 1997; Tiffany, 2006; and http://www.respondentdrivensampling.org/). The method involves not only the typical incentive payment to each study participant, it also involves payment to participants who successfully recruit additional participants (Heckathorn, 1997). Thus, the strategy has significant budgetary implications.

Developing, Producing, and Storing Materials

An array of materials may need to be developed, depending on the planned recruitment and retention activities. The most obvious expense is the production costs for printing posters, flyers, and letters, or recording the visual and audio messages to be distributed. This may involve paying for services such as photography, logo design, videography, audio recording, video and audio editing, and actors. In addition, there may be layout and design costs to take into consideration. Even if project staff do this work, there are costs associated with their time and possibly with software necessary to produce materials of sufficient quality to be effective.

Some of these development activities may be contracted outside of the study team, such as those requiring graphic design, studio recordings of advertising messages, or development of social media materials and a project website. However, the team is going to be responsible for the informational contents of the messages that will be delivered and for developing any professional or community presentations. The team may be developing their own social media messages and e-mail message templates, the time and technology tools for which need to be included in the budgeting process (i.e., computer hardware and software). When working with advertising venues such as radio, television, newspaper, movie theaters, or bus companies, there is likely to be some need to work with their offices to meet their production guidelines. In addition to the creative time and resources, additional resources need to be budgeted to arrange payment for ad development and for working iteratively with their creative development team.

The recruitment and retention materials that are ultimately developed should reflect the lessons learned in chapters 2 and 3 about creating a climate that is interesting, welcoming, and inclusive so as to encourage recruitment and retention: Potential and actual participants must want to participate, and your materials are an important aspect they consider. Once developed and produced, it is possible that storage for the materials that are created needs to be included in the space and equipment budgets (e.g., secure yet accessible locations for printed materials to be stored). Finally, because these recruitment materials are part of the interaction with (potential) participants, they will need to be reviewed by the IRB.

Dissemination

Planning for the dissemination of direct and indirect recruitment messages can be more complex than might initially be expected. First, estimating staff time for oversight of a media campaign (e.g., radio, television, bus, newspaper, and movie ads) can be accomplished by breaking the task into component parts. These might include:

- seeking out the proper contact person/representative for each dissemination outlet,
- meeting with the contact person/representative,
- establishing the placement plan (number of postings/airings, when and why),
- arranging payment for ad placement, and
- ongoing monitoring of the campaign and its effectiveness.

If distribution includes hanging posters or delivering flyers/take away cards, staff will need to budget time to:

- gain management approvals for posting at each desired location,
- deliver the materials,
- conduct periodic inventory of the placed materials, and
- collect leftover materials at recruitment conclusion.

If the media campaign engages social media elements, staff time will need to be dedicated to monitoring those social media sites and messages.

Next, estimating costs associated with dissemination requires a detailed plan related to how many advertisements will be placed, when and where (as costs may vary by time of day/day of week), and length or size of the advertisement. Professional newsletters and publications may have fees associated with placement of notices or advertisements. Sending letters to a professional network costs staff time to assemble, address, and redirect returned mail, as well as the cost of printing, postage, and mailing materials. Hanging posters or delivering flyers to appropriate locations may require travel expenses for the staff distributing them.

In planning the dissemination strategy, it is important to consider when and where the people you are seeking to connect with are likely to see your advertising. In discussing "the seasonality" of recruitment, Danchak (n.d.) presented data suggesting that direct contact methods have comparatively low yield during summer months, at least for medical studies. However, the cost of advertising (radio and television) may be lower, making the overall cost-per-person-recruited more acceptable; spring months tend to have the highest cost-per-person-recruited ratio. Recruitment during holidays may present additional challenges, while recruiting prior to some holidays may enhance the attractiveness of incentive payments (e.g., gift-exchange holidays).

Marketing analysts have large amounts of data and experience related to the peak times when different types of audiences are listening to specific radio stations and watching specific television stations. For example, recruiting among adolescents and emerging adults early in the morning might not be as productive as messages during late afternoon and evening/nighttime hours. Increasingly, marketing demographics are emerging for people engaged in online activities. For example, on-screen advertising can be targeted to the browsing and purchasing histories of users. One piece of marketing advice that may assist in planning your dissemination strategy is that you should strive to have individuals see the advertisements at least three times, in relative proximity, to increase the probability of their recognizing the message and taking action to inquire about the study.

Developing and Implementing the Tracking Systems

In chapter 3 we presented strategies related to participant tracking, including the nature of the information initially collected from participants about themselves and potential key informants. How this information is managed is an important consideration related to tracking effectiveness. Historically, a system of index cards filed by project week or month was a useful tool. The contact information for each participant was placed on a single card. The cards were arranged in sections based on when the next action step was to take place, such as: in study week 3, send a reminder about the scheduled second interview appointment to person A with that same reminder in study week 7 for a different participant enrolled later. Notes about the contact efforts would be marked directly on the index card, such as left a message on (date, time) or reached participant on (date, time) for each effort made. Once the tracking task was accomplished the card would be moved to the proper section for the next activity date. The major limitations to this system are: (1) It is very difficult to retrieve information about an individual participant the way the cards are sorted, and (2) it requires regular monitoring by dedicated staff members to ensure that dates are not overlooked.

Currently, it is possible to use technology to this same effect. A variety of calendar methods are available for computers, smartphones, and tablets with the capability of programming in reminders and alerts. The same sort of tracking information described above is entered for each participant, but the mechanics of scheduling actions are managed by the computer program or app. A simple spreadsheet (e.g., Microsoft Excel) is potentially useful for storing information about individual participants, however it is important to use a system that can easily be sorted or queried by date as well as by participant (e.g., Microsoft Access). Note that studies will benefit from the use of these software packages only if staff receive appropriate training on how to use them effectively.

In addition to how the tracking system is organized, the study team will need to develop the appropriate messages, which relates back to the earlier topic about developing the materials. If the tracking system involves the use of social media, staff will need to dedicate time to monitoring these media and will need templates or scripts for the types of responses they post. These, too, will need to be reviewed by the IRB.

Tracking Through Record Systems

Finally, the investigative team may choose to include a variety of strategies for checking public records (e.g., court and city/county public records), which may be free to use but difficult to learn and are time consuming. Examples include CourtTracker in Wisconsin and eCourts used in the state of New York. Other options include Web-based phone directories (e.g., Switchboard, Lycos People Search, or WhitePages.com), obituary searches, and general resources such as Yahoo Free People Search.

To locate extremely difficult to track participants, the team may elect to "purchase" tracking services from a commercial service (e.g., LexisNexis) or engage a fee-based service with a variety of online people-search services (e.g., Instant Checkmate, Intelius, PeopleFinders). However, a common experience is that the information obtained through these services may be no more accurate or informative than can be obtained with some work applied to (free) public domain sources. And, with some of our more hidden populations, these systems may not work at all. This is when a team may need to plan for some of the "leg-work" methods discussed in chapter 3. It is important that any strategy to be implemented be approved by the IRB and included in the consent process, especially if it involves other than publicly accessible records.

Responding to Inquiries, Prescreening, and Screening

Staff need to be trained and accessible/available to respond to study inquiries as soon as possible when potential participants reach out to the project. While it may seem reasonable to call back on Tuesday after a long holiday weekend, for an individual who initiated contact late on the prior Friday, those intervening days may be too long to wait. The potential participant may have lost the motivation to try your inter-vention, may have found an alternative program in the meantime, or may have lost hope. Given the complicated lives and life structures of the populations with whom we are working, it often is unreasonable to expect their outreach contact efforts to take place during regular busi-ness hours. Therefore, the study team may wish to consider strategies to increase capacity for responding to initial contact efforts to be as close as possible to 24-hour coverage. This may include a rotating system of being "on call," for example.

It helps to recognize the activity patterns of your target population. For example, adolescents tend not to be available before and during school hours, perhaps being more likely to reach out in the late after-noon, evening, and nighttime hours. If study personnel cannot respond immediately when contact is initiated, the outgoing message should provide the potential participant with a time frame within which a response might be expected: before 9 am the following day, for example. It is also possible that the message may need to make reference to time zone if your recruitment materials have been distributed beyond your local region.

Screening Costs

Costs associated with screening of potential participants may include costs associated with the screening tools themselves. Screening may involve biological lab samples with costs including the collection, proper storage, transfer/shipping, and analysis of the samples. Screening may also include the use of licensed or copyright protected measurement tools or clinical assessment protocols that incur fees to reproduce, use, or analyze. Complex screening protocols may require multiple appointments to complete or may be of sufficient length as to require providing food and breaks for the potential participant (and staff). It may be necessary to provide an incentive payment or transportation costs for the screening session, regardless of the screening outcome.

The costs associated with prescreening and screening also may include:

- training staff members to engage effectively in the prescreening/ screening activities (including "re"training when staff turnover occurs and "booster" training to maintain protocol fidelity and reduce "drift");
- monitoring staff members' fidelity to the screening protocol over time;
- keeping staff available to engage in prescreening/screening, e-mail exchanges, or in-person appointments in a timely way, as part of their regular job duties;
- phone or text message charges if a dedicated project line is used or calls are forwarded to "on-call" staff cell phones;
- production or duplication of prescreening/screening information forms, or setting up a computer-assisted screening decision tree;
- personnel time for callbacks and scheduling of screening opportunities;
- electronically scanning and/or secure physical storage of completed screening materials, during and beyond the life of the project (per IRB or other regulatory protocol); and,
- providing screening feedback to potential participants.

Important themes overlying these activities are (1) an awareness of confidentiality and potential Health Information Portability and Accountability Act (HIPAA) regulations regarding how communication about personal physical and behavioral health information might be shared (especially in electronic formats such as texting, e-mails, or record sharing), and (2) that the use of screening technologies may require sophisticated levels of information technology competence or expertise. Finally, the study may have a responsibility for referral-related activities to engage individuals who do not meet the study inclusion criteria, including time to assemble and maintain a referral resource guide and protocol that staff members may follow.

Consenting Potential Participants

We previously referred to consent as a process rather than as an outcome (chapter 2). One cost lies in the time and approaches used in training staff to engage effectively in the process; this includes "re"training efforts when staff turnover occurs and to curtail drift (loss of fidelity) from study protocols.

In the planning for this phase of recruitment, the specific tools to be used in the consent process need to be identified. Consent implies that individual participants have been fully informed about what is expected of them and what they can expect as a result of participating in the study, that they have been provided with ample time to consider the decision and any alternative options, and have had sufficient opportunity to explore any questions they may have. Figured into the study budget must be the time and resources necessary to train project staff to engage consistently and effectively in the consent process.

At the barest minimum, the consent form itself might be the only tool. However, consider the population that you are hoping to recruit and the complexity of the study you are consenting them to join. It may be preferable for a potential participant to be provided with a consent document to take home, carefully review and consider, then return completed. Charts, diagrams, or pictures might be additional helpful tools in the consent process. Showing a brief video on a mobile device might be preferable to reading through pages of text in a consent form. The cost of producing these materials needs to be computed into the project (recruitment) budget. Some costs related to duplicating and securely storing consent materials during and following the study may be eliminated if electronic records of consent are permitted by the IRB. However, many settings are not conducive to the use of the necessary devices: for example, technology is often banned from criminal justice settings, hospital units, and school facilities.

Group consent may be an option to consider, as well. For example, in one study involving women in jails and prisons, we presented the consent information verbally and in writing to a group of assembled women who had expressed an initial interest in participating. Throughout our scripted presentation, the women were encouraged to ask questions and the group could listen to the answers. At the end, women who were not interested or were unwilling to provide consent to participate were welcome to leave the group. Interested women then completed the consent form and were enrolled in the study individually with a member of the study team. Not only was this a relatively efficient method of conveying the information to a large number of individuals but also the women were more comfortable asking questions as a member of a familiar group than in dyads with an unfamiliar investigator.

The importance of recognizing the consent process as part of the working relationship cannot be overstated: participants are considering how it feels to be engaged in the research project at every stage, including the consent process, and this has an impact on not only recruitment but also ongoing retention. Finally, as in the case of individuals who do not meet the study inclusion criteria, the study team members need to have a referral protocol in place for individuals who elect to decline consent but meet criteria for needing services identified in the intervention study.

Enrolling Participants

As noted in chapter 3, study attrition can occur as a result of individuals being disappointed in the result of randomization efforts. For example, a participant may become randomly assigned to a control or treatment as usual (TAU) group when hoping to receive the intervention being tested. Or, vice versa, an individual may have hoped to join the control group and be disappointed with being assigned to a more time- and effort-intensive intervention condition. A well-designed informed consent overview document may help to mitigate against such disappointment (revisit Box 2.4). This document might include questions used to ask potential participants about their thoughts if assigned to one or the other condition. Handling the randomization process with transparency may also help to minimize control group disappointment and reinforce the perception of fairness.

In chapter 1, we briefly mentioned different systems for randomly assigning participants to intervention conditions represented in an intervention study design, with the goal of improving the chances of achieving equivalence between the study groups at the outset. Some suggestions that have relatively high transparency value for participants are worthy of discussion.

Random Number Generators

A variety of tools exist for generating random numbers that can be used in assigning participants to one or another intervention condition. If a finite set of participants has been identified, their identifying information can be entered into a statistical software package in the "wide" format (one participant per line) in the database. SPSS, for example, has a feature in the data menu whereby a set of "cases" can be randomly selected. This subset of individuals can be assigned to one condition and the remaining individuals can be assigned to another. This approach works only if the entire sample is already known, with each individual already holding a known position (line) in the database.

Intervention studies often enroll participants on a rolling basis. In other words, they do not all sign up to participate at once, so the full set of participants is not known until the study is completed. A variation on the theme of generating random numbers is to place participants into the database in order of enrollment, with the assignments for each position in the database already predetermined using a computer-based system of random number generation. For example, a free Web-based resource is located at http://stattrek.com/statistics/random-number-generator.aspx. Generating the numbers requires submission of information about how many random numbers will be needed. If the study design calls for an entire sample of 80 individuals divided into 2 distinct intervention groups of 40 persons in each, this entry would be 40 (to select who is in one group; the unselected numbers will be in the other group). The minimum value could be set as 1 and the maximum value would be 80. The prompt asking about allowing duplicate entries would receive a negative (false) response because you would not want one person to have more than one chance to be entered into the selection. The system then generates 40 random numbers that can be applied to a sequence of enrollment.

The Luck of the Draw, the Roll of the Dice

The use of random number systems can be very precise. Unfortunately, given the uncertainties associated with participant recruitment in intervention studies, we often do not know the exact number of participants we will be able to engage and retain in the study. Therefore, we may need to resort to other strategies for random assignment that may not be quite as precise but still hold promise for creating relatively equal initial groups.

Individuals could draw numbers from a "hat" as they enroll in the study, learning their assignment as they align the number they drew with a posted list of randomly selected numbers. Another randomization technique used in a study with incarcerated women involved the use of Uno cards. We did not know the ultimate number of women to be recruited into the study, but we did know the ratio we wanted assigned to each of two conditions: 2/3 in the new intervention group, 1/3 in the TAU group. We placed each of the red, blue, and green cards into a sealed envelope and each time a participant provided consent to be randomized, she selected an envelope from the collection (which was well mixed each time). The women were informed that red meant the TAU group and either blue or green meant the new intervention group. One advantage of this approach is its transparency. The women knew they had controlled the outcome, that it had not been manipulated in any way by the research team. This was important in managing expectations and disappointment with the random assignment process.

Investigators might consider the use of dice or board game spinners—games of chance. For example, rolling or spinning an odd number places you in one group, an even number in the other. The downside to this sort of "luck of the draw" or "throw of the dice" approach is that it less reliably generates the ratio of assignment that is ultimately desired. The chances of 80 people being perfectly evenly divided into 2 groups of 40 each is low; the potential for a heavily skewed distribution exists, thereby defeating one reason for engaging in randomization in the first place. While transparency works to one's participant retention advantage, it should not overshadow the need to meet the study's design requirements.

Retention Activities

The tracking systems used to maintain contact with participants over the course of a longitudinal intervention study have associated costs. While there may or may not be software expenses associated with establishing and maintaining a tracking database, personnel time and effort are involved. A number of studies in the literature report taking the opportunity to send birthday and holiday greetings to participants, both as a means of maintaining rapport and as an early warning system of address failure: if a card is returned undeliverable, the team knows to engage in targeted tracking activities before scheduled study activities are missed. Another item that might be sent to study participants are brief study updates and reports that maintain a participant's interest and sense of being an important member of the project. For example, sending periodic updates recognizing milestones (e.g., 100 participants enrolled or halfway to the study completion goal) or relating the study's relevance to current events in the news might be helpful, where it is premature to send study results during the study's retention period. Appointment reminder calls, texts, e-mail messages, or letters in the mail are also important to improving the extent to which the study protocol is implemented as designed.

Finally, in the adaptive protocol way of thinking about participant retention, a study team might plan for a range of options related to data collection activities that preserve enough consistency to maintain internal validity and enough flexibility to help maintain study participation. Variation in how the intervention conditions are delivered has less room for flexibility than do the research protocol elements. For example, there may be a data triage plan whereby the first choice is to schedule data collection events during regular business hours; many participants will engage in data collection this way. The second choice might involve making limited, special hours available, such as the occasional weekend or evening time block; this may make participation possible for another group of participants. A third, final option might be to arrange for a data collection visit by team members at a place of convenience for a participant. The third option entails the greatest investment in time and travel expenses, but remains less expensive than losing the participant from the study. In addition, alternative modes of data collection may be employed if there is sufficient evidence in the literature that they are equivalent: telephone interviews, hard copy sent via regular mail with return postage and postal system tracking, or electronic approaches, such as a secure survey tool where images and video clips can be inserted as part of the questions or demonstrations.

BUDGETING FOR PARTICIPANT RECRUITMENT AND RETENTION ACTIVITIES

The previously noted tendency to overestimate the ability to recruit and retain study participants, combined with a tendency to underestimate the costs related to implementing strong recruitment and retention plans, has the potential to create a "perfect storm" leading to study failure. Recruitment and retention costs fall into two general categories: (1) personnel and (2) materials and dissemination fees, many of which have been detailed in the above discussions.

More About Estimating Personnel Costs

While participant recruitment and retention are the responsibility of everyone on a study team, and this might be managed by a committee, it is critically important that leadership and oversight responsibilities reside with one individual. Through experience we have learned that study recruitment and retention can fall too low on the priority list of busy study staff members. A recruitment and retention committee might identify sources and strategies for recruitment, and develop the action blueprint defining who is going to engage in which specific activities, the timelines, and outcome metrics. The lead person would be responsible for directing the decision-making related to progress toward those goals. In this way, study recruitment and retention become a shared, intentional responsibility and less is left to chance.

Involving research personnel in recruitment and retention activities, however, comes at a cost. Participant recruitment and retention processes are time consuming, and the costs of dedicated staff effort must be addressed in a study budget. Unanticipated costs may be associated with training the project staff members to effectively engage in recruitment and retention procedures, activities, and relationships, as well as conforming to IRB protocols. Longitudinal studies might be susceptible to costs of staff attrition and retraining their replacements. Implementing an intention-to-treat design involves intensified tracking and retention effort, since the individuals most likely to drop out of the intervention activities also may be the most difficult to retain in the research protocol.

In some communities and settings, contracting with marketing professionals to help develop recruitment materials and purchase advertising space might be an option to consider. However, paying individuals outside of agency or study staff to engage in participant recruitment is discouraged, and usually violates IRB protocols. For example, Eichenwald and Kolata (1999) reported in the *New York Times* that physicians were being paid "finder's fees" by drug companies for referring their patients to pharmaceutical studies. Presently, many academic institutions and other organizations have policies prohibiting such activity, which can be defined as presenting a conflict of interest. Per a University of Pittsburgh IRB Guidance document, significant ethical conflicts may arise when financial compensation is exchanged for making referrals, meeting enrollment goals, and/or timely study completion (University of Pittsburgh IRB, 2014). Such compensation may influence the individual referring to do so based on compensation versus the best interests of the individual being referred (University of Pittsburgh IRB, 2014). As a result, the University of Pittsburgh IRB Guidance document states that investigators are not allowed to pay finder's fees.

The first step in budgeting for recruitment and retention costs, therefore, relates to developing the most accurate estimates possible for the specific activities in which each team member will be engaged, for how much of their time, for what duration of time, and how much each of those units of time costs. In addition to the time and effort expended in specifying the recruitment plan, members of the team will need to dedicate time and effort to a series of additional recruitment and retention tasks. These tasks are over and above the other research tasks associated with conducting the study, such as:

- delivering the interventions;
- collecting, managing, and analyzing the data;
- reviewing literature;
- writing reports; and,
- maintaining the IRB protocols and amendments.

One technique for estimating personnel costs discussed in the literature for an activity such as prescreening of potential participants is to calculate the time to do the task, then multiply by three times what the administrative costs associated with the activity might be. For example, at 15 minutes for a prescreening telephone call, at $20 per hour, these 15 minutes cost $5; using the administrative cost multiplier of 3 (times the $5) results in a prescreening cost of $15 per person ultimately enrolled.

The assumptions built into this estimate example relate to a fair degree of consistency in the cost of screening across individuals, and the rate at which screened individuals will be enrolled is one out of three.

A sample budget outline dedicated to participant recruitment and retention is presented in Table 4.3; discussed next is a hypothetical example in which recruitment and retention activities occupied 16 months of a 2-year funded project.

Identifying the Target Population

In our hypothetical study the principal investigator ($65/hour), project coordinator ($32.50/hour), and three research assistants (each $20/hour) met for a total of 6 hours on this task. These 6 hours of effort cost $945. In addition, our hypothetical study team decided to conduct two focus groups (11 participants total with $15 incentive payments plus $5 transportation each) that lasted for 1.5 hours each. The project coordinator planned and conducted the group sessions (6 hours total), the research assistants recruited, scheduled, and consented the participants (average 2 hours per participant), and together with the principal investigator they debriefed after the sessions (3-hour meeting). The total cost of the two focus groups was $1,327.50. The project coordinator and principal investigator took turns meeting for an hour each with four community-based programs to become fully informed about the target population and discuss feasibility of the recruitment, intervention, and study protocols. The total cost of these meetings was $195. Liaison activities were part of the general job activities of our hypothetical principal investigator and project coordinator; no additional costs related to recruitment and retention were incurred. *Subtotal: $2,468.*

Identifying Recruitment Options and Distribution Outlets

In addition to 5 planning meetings of 1.5 hours each, dedicated to this topic (total personnel cost at salary rates mentioned above: $881.25), research assistants had assignments to investigate options for radio and bus advertising, hosting a Web page and Facebook identity, as well as producing posters, mailings to referral agencies, and flyers for distribution at referral agencies. They also needed to identify who could provide permission for hanging posters and distributing flyers, and made these contacts to gain the permissions. The cost of this 42 hours of information gathering and report development was $840. The work

Table 4.3 Sample Budget Outline for Recruitment and Retention Activities

Personnel Budget for Recruitment and Retention Activities					
Category for R&R Task/Activity	Person(s)	Hours	Cost/Hour	subtotals	Notes
Prestudy Planning					
identify R&R strategies					
identify targets					
consultation					
liaise with referral agencies					
develop R&R materials					
identify distribution outlets					
submit to IRB					
Implement Plan					
distribution activities					
response to inquiries					
screening/prescreening					
managing social media					
consenting					
enrollment					
tracking participants					
other retention activities					

subtotals

was conducted via telephone, Internet, and e-mail messages, which were all covered under the university services, and no travel was involved, although long-distance telephone calls totaled $254. *Subtotal: $1,975.*

Developing Recruitment and Retention Materials
The team worked together to develop the recruitment message content based on the focus group feedback ($481.25 in meeting and independent work time). A graphic design person developed the layout for the posters, flyers, mailings, and a logo for the project based on the feedback from the focus groups and the project team. This work was performed as a "match" from the university (estimated match cost $2,800). The bus advertisement layouts were developed as part of the advertising contract with the bus service (see next section). The radio advertisements cost a total of $600 to professionally record. Design of the project Web page and Facebook identity required 10 hours of project assistant time ($200). Printing costs for the posters, flyers, mailings, and printed adhesive Post-it notes with study contact information on the posters totaled $2,655 (including envelopes) and 4 hours of research assistant time ($80) to assemble. Submitting all materials to the IRB for approval required approximately 5 hours of project coordinator time ($162.50). *Subtotal: $4,179.*

Dissemination
The radio advertising contract for the number of advertisement airings, at the times recommended by the marketing experts was $6,500. The bus advertising contract for the number of postings on the specified routes, during the time period recommended by the marketing experts, was $6,200. The direct mailing effort budget included $2,400 in postage, and research assistant time to hand address the mailing was estimated at 5 hours ($100); first-class postage and hand-addressed envelopes are recommended in the literature as a means of increasing the likelihood that mail will be read rather than discarded (e.g., the Dillman total design method; Dillman, 1978). Travel for research assistants to deliver, monitor, replace, and collect the posters and flyers throughout the recruitment period of the study was budgeted at 75 hours ($1,500) and $2,800 for their mileage reimbursement. The Web page was hosted by the university without charge to the project, and the Facebook presence was also free of charge. *Subtotal: $19,500.*

Respond to Inquiries, Screening/Prescreening

The project team had a person "on call" to respond to telephone and electronic inquiries about the project from 7 am to midnight, 7 days a week, for the duration of the recruitment and retention period (16 months of the 2-year study). The project coordinator's and research assistants' regular work schedules were staggered to cover the 7 am to 7 pm period, hence their availability to respond to inquiries was not considered an additional cost. [Additional costs associated with taking calls from 7 pm to midnight would be for a total of 2,400 hours during the 16-month period of recruitment. Since funders are unlikely to cover this "on call" expense, it is not included in the budget. However, investigators need to make staff aware that these hours are part of their regular paid duties. And, these responsibilities are distinct from the clinical call duties assumed by those who delivered the intervention.]

A total of 1,213 potential participants were engaged in screening for possible enrollment in the study (see CONSORT diagram, Figure 5.1, in chapter 5). The screening interviews were conducted by telephone and required 15–60 minutes, depending on the responses received, scheduling a baseline data collection visit, and record keeping; the average time for the 128 not meeting inclusion criteria was 20 minutes (43 hours), for the 29 who declined participation was 45 minutes (22 hours), and for completed interviews was 60 (1,056 hours). The total time spent in screening activities was 1,121 hours at a total personnel cost of $26,560 for a mixture of project coordinator and research assistant time. Training these individuals to conduct the screening interviews and maintaining/monitoring their fidelity to the screening interview protocol required 100 hours over the course of the study (combined efforts from principal investigator, project coordinator, and research assistant trainees) for a total cost of $1,600. The screening tools were all in the public domain, so there were no costs associated with their use. The information was entered into a database through a Qualtrics "survey" by the staff member conducting the screening interview. *Subtotal: $28,160.*

Manage Social Media Presence

A total of 5 hours per week for the 70-week recruitment and retention phase were dedicated for research assistants to manage the social media presence of the project. *Subtotal: $7,000.*

Consenting and Enrolling Participants

The project coordinator and research assistants shared in these responsibilities. The consent process and random assignment to study condition were scheduled for 60 minutes per participant ($N = 1,010$). In addition, scheduling these appointments and participants' missed appointments totaled another 950 hours, and training the staff to engage in these consent and enrollment protocols required another 10 hours that included some of the principal investigator's time. *Subtotal: $46,250.*

Tracking Participants

Research assistants were occupied with both usual and enhanced tracking and retention activities throughout the 16-month recruitment and retention phase of the project. This included telephone, e-mail, or text message reminders about appointments, per each participant's preferred method of notification. It also included Web-based searches for updated locator information about individuals who had moved or with whom connection lapsed. Tracking the 1,010 participants required a total of 1,800 hours. *Subtotal: $36,000.*

Total Impact

The total budgetary impact of the study recruitment and retention plan was $145,532. This does not include the costs of delivering the intervention or collecting the study data, nor any of the costs associated with data management, analysis, and reporting.

The costs would not be represented quite this way in a typical grant proposal budget; instead the personnel costs would be folded into general categories for hourly and salary personnel that include the entire job each will be hired to complete. The example is helpful in two ways, however. The first is that it demonstrates the myriad tasks to consider in planning for participant recruitment and retention, as well as the time that will be necessary to consider in each individual's overall effort on the project. Second, it allows us to demonstrate the high budgetary costs associated with the loss of each study participant who is initially enrolled. In our hypothetical study, a total of 211 participants were "lost to follow-up" over the course of the study. Each of those individuals cost approximately $28 to initially recruit, $75 to screen, and $81 to enroll. At a minimum the loss of each of these individuals amounted to $184, for a total loss of $38,824 to the project. Additional losses are associated with the cost of delivering any portion of the intervention and any incentive payments made along the way before study dropout occurred. And, the potential loss to the study's integrity is not calculated in dollars.

COST-EFFECTIVENESS ANALYSES

Final resources to aid investigators in developing their participant recruitment and retention plans is information related to the cost-effectiveness of different strategies and how a study team can begin to analyze cost-effectiveness of their own strategies to inform future studies. To begin, the yield of a specific strategy in terms of how many study participants are generated can be related to cost of using that strategy. First, investigators may consider the relationship between recruitment and retention dollars (RRD) and study effectiveness in number of participants enrolled (PE). In other words, the participant enrollment cost (PEC) is reflected in a ratio where the cost of recruitment and retention is in the numerator and the number of participants fully enrolled in the study is in the denominator:

$$PEC = RRD/PE$$

Reports of recruitment cost-effectiveness are necessary in order to allow investigators to systematically approach the challenges of budgeting for participant recruitment and retention. Although some published reports on the cost-effectiveness of specific participant recruitment methods exist in the intervention research literature (e.g., Baigis, Francis, & Hoffman, 2003; Gill, McGloin, Gahbauer, Shepard, & Bianco, 2001), the overall number of these reports is relatively small. It helps to keep in mind, however, that cost-effectiveness analysis of this sort is not a perfect science. The effects of time, advertising costs, changes in media message content, and other changes such as advertisement placement and scheduled airtime may influence the overall cost-effectiveness of specific recruitment methods.

In planning a new study, investigators can use this information to estimate the recruitment and retention costs per study participant, multiply that figure by the number of participants needed to fulfill the study design, and end up with a total estimate for participant recruitment and retention. This is where estimating the rate of participant loss at each point in the process becomes important and informative. For example:

- How many individuals need to respond initially to recruitment efforts in order to generate the necessary number of prescreening/screening events?
- How many screening events need to occur in order to generate the necessary consent procedures (ratio of screening per enrolled participant)?
- How many potential participants engaged in consent will agree and move into study enrollment?

Eventually, investigators will need to be able to estimate how many need to be enrolled in order to complete the study with integrity. All of the associated costs contribute to estimating the recruitment/retention cost per participant.

Recruitment Yield Analysis

In addition to the study's PEC ratio, investigators may find two additional ratios reported in the literature. One is the recruitment yield effectiveness (RYE), which reflects the amount of benefit gained for applying a specific recruitment strategy as a result of the effort expended. The other is recruitment yield cost-effectiveness (RYC), which translates the RYE into research dollars (Baigis et al., 2003; Gill et al., 2001). The advantage of using the RYE and RYC over the PEC ratio alone is that they provide a more detailed breakdown of the process. While the PEC ratio is based on the overall cost associated with the number of participants actually enrolled in a study, the RYE is indicative of the number enrolled using a particular recruitment strategy. In other words, how many individuals contacted the study team, or perhaps how many were prescreened/screened as a result of that specific recruitment strategy, and of those, how many were actually enrolled in the study as a result? And, the RYC assesses the cost associated with that yield.

RYE = (recruitment responses)/(enrolled participants)
RYC = (cost in dollors)/(enrolled participants)

A mathematically tricky situation emerges when no recruited participants are actually enrolled as a result, since a zero denominator creates an impossible ratio. Therefore, it is simplest to assume that the overall RYE reflects a failed effort (RYE = 0), despite there having been potential participants recruited.

Although highly related, the RYE and RYC ratios differentially inform investigators about the overall cost-effectiveness of various participant recruitment strategies and methods. For example, in relation to other methods, a specific method may appear to be more cost-effective in dollars spent (RYC). Yet, the method may have proven more "costly" in other ways. For example, if the method produced a large number of phone calls from ineligible individuals compared to calls from eligible and eventually enrolled participants (RYE), the method's cost-effectiveness must be considered relative to the time and effort spent by study personnel in triaging calls from ineligible individuals. Such considerations can (and probably should) be taken into account by adding additional staffing costs plus other available related costs (e.g., staff time and travel in implementing the recruitment strategy) into the numerator of the RYC ratio.

Table 4.4 presents data related to the cost-effectiveness of different approaches used at one locale in multisite intervention studies recruiting individuals meeting specific criteria for an alcohol use disorder. One question asked at the initial brief screening contact was how the participants heard about the study, what made them call. In this example, newspaper advertising was quite effective in terms of productivity: this strategy resulted in 17 participants being enrolled. However, the cost per

Table 4.4 Study Cost-Effectiveness Analysis, Example A

Recruitment Method	Direct Cost	Participant Yield	Cost per Participant
Bus Placards	$1,000	2	$500
Newsletters	$0	17	$0
Newspaper Ads	$3,667	17	$216
Other Referral	?	10	?
Posters/Flyers	$125	0	No Yield
Press Releases	$0	4	$0
Provider Referral	$0	13	$0
Radio Ads	$2,393	10	$239
Television Ads	$5,355	31	$173
Television News	$0	21	$0
Unknown	?	8	?
Total	$12,540	133	$95

participant was considerable compared to another strategy that resulted in an equal number of enrolled participants at no cost: that being publishing announcements in newsletters. Disappointing was the total failure of posters and flyers to recruit any participants despite the cost. The single most productive approach was the television advertising, generating 31 participants. The greatest success in terms of cost per participant were observed with press releases and television news briefings about the project responding to an important social problem affecting the community. Together these attracted 25 participants at zero cost.

Additional data and analyses specific to the different mass-media strategies used in this example are presented in Table 4.5, including both RYE and RYC outcomes. Television advertising proved to be the most efficient in terms of staff time, as it attracted a high proportion of eligible compared to ineligible participants once screening efforts were taken into consideration. In addition, television advertising was the most effective method in enrolling both women and racial/ethnic minorities into the study. While television advertising was the most expensive strategy of all those employed, the cost per participant was less than for newspaper, bus, and radio advertising.

As a point of contrast, Table 4.6 presents similar information from a different study recruiting a different population. These data are from an HIV-risk reduction intervention (Heart to Heart) for women with an alcohol use disorder. In this analysis, the single most productive strategy was posting flyers in the communities where these women live, work, shop, and recreate. The approach generated 23 study participants at a cost of under $17 each. The mail campaign to homes in the target neighborhoods was very expensive overall and in terms of the yield: recruitment through this means cost over $6,800 for each of the 2 women it brought into the study. The referral network was, again, a very cost-effective mechanism. At no cost per participant, 21 participants were enrolled.

Results of these RYE and RYC analyses may or may not be the same across subgroups recruited into a study, as they are for the study considered as a whole. One approach may be more cost-effective than another for different demographic groups, for example. Furthermore, investigators may have a different value placed on overall recruitment yield than on diversity or cost-effectiveness, leading them to develop different priorities for the various options. Assessing which approaches are most desirable requires a combination of decisions that hopefully

Table 4.5 Detailed Analyses for Media Recruitment Methods from Example A

Recruitment Media Methods	RYE[a]	RYC[b] ($)	Additional Cost RYC[c] ($)	Women[d] (%)	Racial/Ethnic Minorities[e] (%)
Bus Placards	12/2 = 6	1000/2 = 500	1114/2 = 557	0	0
Newspaper Ads	51/17 = 3	3667/17 = 216	4053/17 = 238	11.4	11.7
Posters/Flyers	0	No Yield (125)	No Yield (159)	0	0
Radio Ads	32/10 = 3.2	2393/10 = 239	2643/10 = 264	11.4	11.1
Television Ads	116/31 = 3.7	5355/31 = 173	6321/31 = 204	25.0	38.7

[a]RYE = (number of prescreened callers generated from each media method) ÷ (number of participants enrolled/randomized); note that posters/flyers generated three prescreen callers with no successful enrollments.

[b]RYC = (direct advertising US dollar costs of each media method) ÷ (number of participants enrolled/randomized)

[c]Additional cost RYC ratio also contains in the numerator the average *unweighted* staffing costs associated with the routine telephone prescreening (30 minute interview) of one ineligible study participant (estimated cost $11.36) multiplied by the number of prescreened ineligible callers produced by the media method; for more specificity, the costs could be *weighted* on the basis of differences in effort (and therefore cost) associated with staff members in different positions.

[d]Percentage of participants enrolled/randomized into the study from each media method who were women.

[e]Percentage of participants enrolled/randomized into the study from each media method who were racial/ethnic minorities (defined as nonwhite participants).

Table 4.6 Cost-Effectiveness Analysis, Example B

Recruitment Method	Direct Cost	Participant Yield	Cost/Participant
AODA Provider	$0	13	$0
Non-AODA Provider	$0	8	$0
Bus Placards	$1,500	1	$1,500
Flyer	$382.50	23	$16.63
Mail Campaign	$13,672	2	$6835.88
Word of Mouth	$0	10	$0
Total	$15,555	57	$273

are informed by data. In the end, the use of multiple, diverse types of approaches may be required to fully enroll participants in an intervention study; the purpose of these analyses is to help investigators develop a triaged plan whereby the most promising approaches are employed first, leaving the higher risk strategies for later in the process. The analyses, being largely post hoc, can aid in monitoring study resource utilization and help plan for resource needs and recruitment strategies in future studies.

Use of Analytics

Investigators may have access to various analytic tools associated with social media. For example, analytics such as Ad Manager in Facebook and Twitonomy can be used to monitor the recruitment effectiveness of these social media platforms by tracking the number of ad clicks and number of retweets, respectively (Resko et al., 2017). Couper et al. (2010) described a technological approach to behavioral studies where both the intervention and data collection occur via the Internet. In addition to outcome data, they used process data from participants' Internet interactions (e.g., amount and location of time spent), using what is referred to as *paradata*. In some online delivery platforms, *metadata* are accessible for providing more complex, subtle information about participants' engagement with the materials. For our purposes, it is possible that paradata and metadata may help inform investigators about factors related to participant retention, as well.

CHAPTER SUMMARY

In this chapter we presented a number of tools and resources related to planning for and analyzing recruitment and retention of participants in intervention studies. We first addressed skills and issues related to identifying participant recruitment/retention goals to fit a specific study design and satisfy the demands of specified statistical analytic approaches to be applied to the data. This process of determining sample size, including diversity and subgroup representation, occurs during the initial study planning process and informs many of the subsequent steps in the recruitment and retention process. Next, we presented a sequenced list of the steps that might be taken in planning for effective participant recruitment and retention. These steps relate back to the contents presented in chapters 1, 2, and 3. The discussion here further develops some of the more nuanced issues that investigators may wish to take into consideration in planning for successful participant recruitment and retention. The remainder of the chapter demonstrated aspects of budgeting for the time and other resources necessary in the implementation of a strong participant recruitment and retention plan. The resources presented in these final two sections assist in planning for and monitoring the resources related to a specific study, but also provide a framework for completed studies to help inform the planning of future studies.

5

Final Recommendations and Conclusions

This final chapter covers two topics. The first is a discussion of what investigators might consider as options for assessing aspects of their recruitment and retention outcomes, and how these outcomes might affect results related to the study's tested hypotheses. The discussion includes a general orientation to statistical approaches for addressing recruitment or retention issues that may arise. The final new topic in this book addresses how investigators might present information about recruitment and retention outcomes for their intervention or evaluation studies in manuscripts, presentations, and reports.

ASSESSING AND ADDRESSING RECRUITMENT/RETENTION OUTCOMES

First and foremost, we want to reemphasize that using all feasible options for ensuring strong recruitment and retention is *always* preferable to the compensatory alternatives. These recruitment and retention options and issues are discussed throughout the first four chapters of this book. However, we also recognize that because study recruitment and retention goals are not easily achieved, there may be circumstances where alternative strategies might warrant consideration. These data assessment and analytic strategies may help address internal and/or external validity concerns that might arise as a result of problematic recruitment or retention.

Assessing Sampling Error

Even the best efforts at drawing, recruiting, and retaining a sample from the population can fail to adequately represent that population. There is always an element of chance involved, and the potential for systematic bias, to influence sampling outcomes—and thus, the outcomes of an intervention study. Our earlier demonstration (chapter 1) about the relationship between sample size and population representativeness suggests one factor that investigators can manage through proper study design and the application of strong participant recruitment and retention strategies.

Other issues can be managed through carefully planned and implemented recruitment efforts across the studied population, as well as minimizing retention-related selection bias. For example, investigators may opt to employ deliberate oversampling strategies, such as disproportionate or stratified sampling, to ensure adequate representation of specific population subgroups in the study.

An important study design decision that needs to be made at the outset of planning concerns whether the study sample should represent a population's distribution on a particular variable or whether there is a need for overrepresentation of a subgroup in order to adequately test the intervention or evaluation study hypotheses. For example, examining how results differ by gender is a common intervention research question, therefore attempts to recruit equal proportions of men and women are often seen in research sampling designs. However, in studying patterns and barriers to engaging services during community reentry following release from incarceration, the equal-proportions design was only one option we considered: to recruit men and women in approximately the same distribution reflected in the jail and prison population, which is between 8% and 11% women. However, one of our study hypotheses concerned differences in services accessed by men and women. Thus, we elected to recruit a larger-than-representative sample of women because the approximately 10% of women in the total sample would not allow confident statistical comparisons by gender (Begun, Early, & Hodge, 2016). Disproportionate or stratified sampling efforts are an important consideration whenever there exists disproportionate representation in study-relevant characteristics, either singly or in combination, across the population of individuals (e.g., race, ethnicity, sexual orientation, diagnostic criteria, or age group).

In the end, investigators are left with the need to address the question: How well did those participants engaged in the study represent the population or subgroups in the population to whom study results will be generalized? Answering this question is easily accomplished if the statistical parameters on the variables of interest for the population are known: knowing the population mean and standard deviation (variance) on a specific variable allows for an accurate assessment of the sampling error for those parameters. However, since social work or behavioral health intervention studies often involve variables for which these population parameters are unknown, and working through the methods in detail is beyond the scope of this book, we refer readers to the myriad statistical training sources available in textbooks, courses, and online resources available for assessing sampling error in these situations.

What we can cover is where investigators might look for possible sources of sample bias. First, reliance on convenience (nonprobability) samples is potentially problematic: if we only include in our sample those individuals who are readily and conveniently accessible, we risk a significant source of bias. For example, an intervention study might include only individuals who can attend intervention sessions during normal business hours. As a result, systematically excluded from the sample would be individuals who are in school, lack work schedule flexibility, or lack childcare during these hours.

Reliance on convenience samples of university student subject pools has long been a topic of concern raised in the literature. Similarly, criticism has been voiced about relying on clinical populations alone to test study hypotheses: the results are generalizable only to individuals who successfully obtained patient or client status, not the more heterogeneous population of individuals for whom an intervention might be designed. For example, the intervention may be tested only on individuals sufficiently motivated to seek participation in the intervention study and may not work in the same way with individuals who are mandated to receive the treatment or who have other treatment options available.

Selection bias may also be the result of biased response or systematic nonresponse by clinicians relied on to provide data about their client populations or who may be involved in referring potential participants to the study (see Gerstein & Johnson, 2000 analysis). For example, they may only refer their most difficult clients with whom they do not expect to achieve a good treatment outcome themselves, leading to a sample biased around symptom or co-occurring diagnosis. Or, they may only refer clients without the means to pay for services, leading to a socioeconomic bias.

A study might suffer bias resulting from undercoverage of the population for whom the interventions are designed. For example, imagine a study designed to prevent unintended pregnancy among adolescents and emerging adults. Now imagine that the sampling approach results in inclusion only of individuals over the age of 16 years. This could happen either directly through the use of an age-related exclusion criterion or indirectly through the use of other enrollment criteria that unintentionally restrict the inclusion of persons younger than 16 in the study. The result is a study where the intervention remains untested with the underrepresented 12- to 15-year-old population. Thus, it is important to determine the degree of heterogeneity across the population of interest and assess the extent to which the full range of individuals for whom the intervention is intended is being successfully recruited and retained.

If we rely on word-of-mouth and "snowball" sampling strategies, without the kind of social network controls built into respondent-driven sampling methods, heterogeneity in our sample is threatened through the principle of *homophily*. This principle suggests that people tend to build and retain social connections, or affiliate, with others who are "like" themselves, not so much with people who are markedly different. Thus, without concerted, organized efforts being applied, a study sample generated this way could end up without sufficient diversity: various groups may be underrepresented, ultimately reducing the study's external validity.

Random Assignment Adequacy

Like recruitment from a population, our best efforts at randomly assigning enrolled participants to different intervention condition groups are subject to elements of chance. The distribution in our comparison groups may be quite satisfactory along many dimensions (e.g., gender, age, race, and ethnicity) but not all relevant dimensions (e.g., problem severity, diagnostic characteristics, or motivation to change). Investigators often conduct initial statistical comparison analyses to test the null hypothesis of no group differences prior to conducting analyses for testing the actual study hypotheses. In these instances, we are hoping that the analyses result in "fail to reject the null hypothesis" decisions—a hope that students of research sometimes find difficult to grasp.

For example, a 2 × 2 chi-square analysis could be used to determine if the subgroups randomly assigned to a new treatment versus treatment as usual (TAU) condition were similar in terms of the proportion receiving extreme-positive Alcohol Use Disorder Identification Test (AUDIT) scores at study intake (i.e., scores over 16, where any score over 8 is positive). In this case, an investigator would hope not to reject the null hypothesis that the proportion of participants with extreme scores in the two treatment groups is equal (i.e., that $p > .05$ and the 95% confidence interval includes zero). In other words, the possibility remains that the two comparison groups are evenly divided on this dimension and that the random assignment effort was successful as far as that particular variable was concerned.

What if our analysis showed, however, that the two groups were not initially distributed as we had hoped when we applied our random assignment strategy? We discover the problem only after the study is completed. We could panic over this randomization failure, but that would not be productive. Instead, one option is to analyze the study data somewhat differently. Perhaps, rather than comparing outcome data for everyone in each of the two groups, it might be worthwhile to conduct analyses where each individual in the intervention group is matched one-to-one with a similar individual in the comparison group. Participant matching takes place along the variable (or variables) of greatest potential impact on the study outcomes. Dattalo (2010) discusses this as the "constructed comparison group" strategy.

This participant matching strategy works reasonably well when the number of important factors (covariates) is limited. As the number of variables increases, the complexity of matching pairs of individuals becomes increasingly difficult. The inability to find matched pairs can severely limit the sample size included in final analyses, and thus reduce statistical power. This is especially important for intervention studies, which for many reasons (e.g., participant risk/burden or recruitment/ retention expense) tend to propose recruitment of "just enough" participants to attain adequate statistical power for the detection of significant effects. Propensity score matching allows for inclusion of pairs matched on as many of the key selected variables as possible: it is more forgiving than a fully matched strategy, identifying the best matches possible without requiring a match on every variable. Propensity score matching also is discussed by Dattalo (2010). This approach can help to reduce the impact of sample bias in the interpretation of treatment effects, as it accounts for covariates that may predict receipt versus nonreceipt of an intervention (Guo, Barth, & Gibbons, 2004). Propensity score matching can also be used to implement simulated "randomized" conditions using nonexperimental data (e.g., Barth, Gibbons, & Guo, 2006; Barth, Guo, & McCrae, 2007).

Missing Data Solutions

Just as recruitment and random assignment may not proceed as planned, data completion efforts may encounter difficulties, as well. Before discussing missing data solutions, however, we wish to emphasize an essential point: applying statistical analytic techniques is a poor substitute for proper study design and execution, and may not be able to correct for biases due to data loss (Lauby et al., 1996). However, the best-laid plans may go awry, leaving investigators faced with missing data dilemmas.

The solutions adopted depend on (1) the amount of missing data and (2) the nature of the "missingness." Data may be randomly missing, where various participant responses are missing throughout the dataset in nonsystematic ways. This might either be random across all variables and participants in the study, or it might be random within only certain subgroups in the sample (Dattalo, 2010; Diaz-Ordaz, Kenward, Cohen, Coleman, & Eldridge, 2014).

Unfortunately, the opposite is all too often the case: data are missing in systematic ways. For example, in our study of incarcerated mothers' responses to a 69-item childcare opinions questionnaire, a large number of respondents quit before completing the final page of items. Generally this might be an indication of respondent burden. In this case, however, the problem was that many of the surveys were distributed on "Commissary Day" when women had a single, twice-monthly opportunity to purchase personal care and food items, and their window of opportunity was only open when their names were called. Thus, many of our participants left unfinished materials, making the missing data systematic in nature: the latter parts were missing more than the earlier parts.

Seeking the source of missing data is also discussed in the literature as an important process in which to engage (Schwartz & Beaver, 2014). Various strategies for handling missing data are discussed in the literature, along with some discussion of their limitations (e.g., Dattalo, 2010; Molenberghs, et al., 2015; Sterne et al., 2009). These missing data issues and approaches apply to many types of research; however, missing data due to study attrition is a special case with significance to longitudinal study designs, such as those often used in intervention and evaluation research.

Intention-to-Treat Analysis

In behavioral intervention studies using a longitudinal design, retention failure is a common cause for missing data. Intention-to-treat (ITT) strategies and analyses provide a means of improving the accuracy and generalizability of interpretations drawn from intervention study outcomes. Intention-to-treat analyses take into account all available data for retained and nonretained participants alike, rather than excluding nonretained individuals from the intervention outcome analyses because of incomplete data. Intention-to-treat analysis represents a more conservative approach for interpreting intervention effectiveness than analyses that only include participants who complete an entire study protocol (Gupta, 2011; Hollis & Campbell, 1999; Little & Kang, 2015; Richy & Mawet, 2007). Results that include only those who complete the protocol as originally planned may overinflate the impact of the intervention, making it seem more effective than was actually the case when all participants' experiences are analyzed—especially considering that participants who "drop out" are likely to have characteristics that differ from those who complete the intervention.

In planning for ITT analyses, project staff members may need to be trained to realize that even if participants decide not to continue with intervention procedures they should still be encouraged to continue with completing research assessments. Follow-up with these participants may be challenging and uncomfortable for research teams, as there may be many possible reasons for someone leaving the study. However, data from these participants can be used in an ITT design during study analyses, and it is vital that the outcome data are collected from as many participants as possible, even if they are no longer interested in attending the intervention. In one study, we encountered an experience where a project's frontline staff did not know that these participants could continue with research assessment (data collection activities); with training, they were able to prevent participants' attrition out of the intervention procedures from also becoming participant attrition out of the remainder of the study protocol. As a result, ITT analyses became possible.

REPORTING RECRUITMENT AND RETENTION OUTCOMES

Currently, several models exist for reporting detailed results concerning the pattern of recruitment and retention in intervention and other types of research studies. Not only do these enrich the report but also they help inform future studies and are crucial to meta-analytic approaches used in systematic review of related intervention studies. As social work and behavioral health research fields evolve, reviewers and editors more and more are requesting or requiring the inclusion of this type of information for intervention studies. The dilemma is that journal space/word limits often preclude this level and type of detail.

Examples of models directed at increasing the transparency of reporting about participant recruitment and retention data include:

- Preferred Reporting Items for Systematic-reviews and Meta-Analyses (PRISMA),
- STrengthening the Reporting of OBservations Studies in Epidemiology (STROBES),
- Transparent Reporting of Evaluations with Nonrandomized Designs (TREND) statements,
- QUality of Reporting of Meta-Analyses (QUOROM), and
- CONsolidated Standards of Reporting Trials (CONSORT).

Since about 1996, medical journals have increasingly endorsed the application of CONSORT guidelines in the reporting about clinical trials. More recently, editors in the social and behavioral intervention literature are adopting the sort of guidelines implemented in medical journals, raising the expectation that investigators are able to report this sort of detailed information. Greater transparency includes details concerning the nature of the interventions being tested, as well as a study's recruitment and retention processes and outcomes (Grant et al., 2013). The hope is that greater transparency will help answer internal and external validity questions with strong implications for study integrity as discussed in chapter 1. It is also worth noting that recruitment into an intervention study may differ markedly from how individuals gain access to services outside of a study context (Grant et al., 2013). This has implications for the implementation science phase of knowledge building about the interventions under study.

Here we have elected to demonstrate reporting about study participation patterns with the CONSORT diagram. Elements of a standardized trial report generally include information concerning participant eligibility criteria, how sample size was determined, recruitment numbers, how participants were randomized to the different conditions under study, whether participants were "blinded" to the condition, the numbers of participants randomized to each condition or group, numbers of participants included in analyses for each condition or group, participant attrition (and reasons) for each condition or group, ancillary analyses related to subgroups, trial limitations potentially affecting bias (internal validity), and generalizability (external validity) of the study results (www.consort-statement.org/checklists/view/32-consort/67-abstract). The CONSORT flow diagram is a useful summary tool. A hypothetical example can help demonstrate its utility: The visual diagram is a more parsimonious format for representing this information than is the written text below (see Figure 5.1).

CONSORT Flow Diagram (Hypothetical) Example

Imagine an intervention study that compares two 8-week treatment conditions (contingency management, or CM, and cognitive-behavioral therapy, CBT) for the management of binge drinking among college freshmen. First, we would discuss enrollment patterns for the study. If

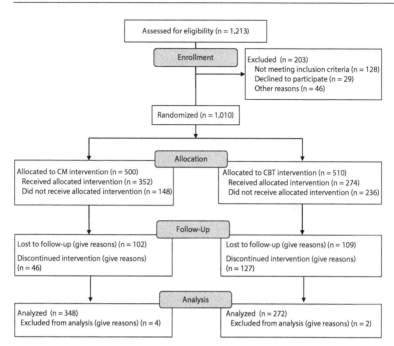

Figure 5.1 CONSORT Diagram Example for Hypothetical Intervention Study

campus recruitment generated responses from 1,213 students, this is entered as the number initially assessed for eligibility—all individuals who responded to our recruitment efforts. Imagine that we administered a brief telephone screening instrument and found that 128 of those responding did not meet the study inclusion criteria (aged 18 and above, engaged in binge drinking during the past month, and in good academic standing). Next, 29 individuals declined to participate once they engaged in the consent process, and 46 failed to show up for their baseline and randomization appointments. This leaves us with 1,010 enrolled participants to randomize into our two comparison conditions.

The allocation phase of the flow chart depicts the numbers randomized to each condition. The result of our randomization efforts is relatively even, though not perfectly so (500 vs. 510). After the eight weeks, we see a distinct difference in the number of individuals who completed the two intervention programs: The CM intervention fared much better than did CBT. In our report we would be responsible for explaining why

148 students dropped out of the CM condition and why 236 dropped out of the CBT condition (e.g., got bored with it, got too busy, no longer eligible because they dropped out of school, became hospitalized or incarcerated). We might learn this from concerted efforts to follow-up with these individuals and ask about their attrition from the intervention (not from the study), and we would also report those who were lost to follow-up from the study. Finally, we look at the analysis phase of the flow chart. In our hypothetical example, 348 members of the CM treatment group and 272 of the CBT group provided complete data of sufficient quality to be included in the outcome analyses; however, anyone from whom baseline data were collected, leading to randomization, would be included in ITT analysis. We would need to describe why data from four members of the CM group and two members of the CBT group were not included in the analyses (e.g., the audio recordings were unintelligible, missing data exceeded our 10% criterion point for inclusion). Ideally, the CONSORT diagram would be presented as part of our manuscript rather than the lengthy text above that we used to explain it.

CHAPTER SUMMARY

In conclusion, many strategies and approaches promote strong participant recruitment and retention in intervention and evaluation research. Assessing the strength of the final study sample is an important process, preceding analysis of outcome data. Investigators should consider strategies for monitoring and addressing the potential problems during the study planning and implementation phases. A few alternatives might be possible after data collection is complete; however, these compensatory strategies are never as desirable as successful recruitment and retention in the first place. Finally, investigators have tools, such as the CONSORT diagram to help succinctly describe the recruitment and retention outcomes of study. It is important for this sort of information to be included in manuscripts, presentations, and reports to facilitate future project planning, including by other investigators working in similar areas or with similar populations, as well as for facilitating systematic and meta-analytic reviews.

References

Abadie, R. (2010). *The professional guinea pig: Big Pharma and the risky world of human subjects*. Durham, NC: Duke University Press.

Alston, M., & Bowles, W. (2013). *Research for social workers* (3rd ed.). New York, NY: Routledge.

American Psychological Association (APA). (2009). *Publication manual of the American Psychological Association* (6th ed.). Washington, DC: American Psychological Association.

Andersen, E. (2007). Participant retention in randomized, controlled trials: The value of relational engagement. *International Journal for Human Caring, 11*(4), 46–51.

Armistead, L. P., Clark, H., Barber, C. N., Dorsey, S., Hughley, J., Favors, M., & Wyckoff, S. C. (2004). Participant retention in the Parents Matter! program: Strategies and outcomes. *Journal of Child and Family Studies, 13*(1), 67–80.

Association of College and Research Libraries (ACRL). (n.d.). *Social work liaison's toolkit: Data sets*. Retrieved from http://www.ala.org/acrl/aboutacrl/directoryofleadership/sections/ebss/ebsswebsite/socialworksocialwelfare/toolkit/data.

Attkisson, C. C., & Zwick, R. (1982). The Client Satisfaction Questionnaire: Psychometric properties and correlations with service utilization and psychotherapy outcome. *Evaluation and Program Planning, 5*, 233–237.

Austin, M.-P., Colton, J., Priest, S., Reilly, N., & Hadzi-Pavlovic, D. (2013). The Antenatal Risk Questionnaire (ANRQ): Acceptability and use for psychosocial risk assessment in the maternity setting. *Women and Birth, 26*(1), 17–25. doi: 10.1016/j.wombi.2011.06.002

Barth, R. P., Gibbons, C., & Guo, S. (2006). Substance abuse treatment and the recurrence of maltreatment among caregivers with children living at home: A propensity score analysis. *Journal of Substance Abuse Treatment, 30,* 93–104.

Barth, R. P., Guo, S., & McCrae, J. S. (2007). Propensity score matching strategies for evaluating the success of child and family service programs. *Research on Social Work Practice, 18,* 212–222.

Begun, A. L. (*2016*). Considering the language we use: Well worth the effort. *Journal of Social Work Practice in the Addictions, 16*(3), 332–336.

Begun, A. L., Berger, L. K., & Salm-Ward, T. (2011). Using a lifecourse context for exploring alcohol change attempts and treatment efforts among individuals with alcohol dependency. *Journal of Social Work Practice in the Addictions, 11,* 101–123.

Begun, A. L., Early, T. J., & Hodge, A. I. (2016). Mental health and substance abuse service engagement by men and women during community reentry following incarceration. *Administration and Policy in Mental Health and Mental Health Services Research, 43,* 207–218.

Begun, A. L., & Gregoire, T. (2014). *Conducting substance use research*. Pocket Guides to Social Work Research. New York, NY: Oxford University Press.

Bell, K. R., Hammond, F., Hart, T., Bickett, A. K., Temkin, N. R., & Dikmen, S. (2008). Participant recruitment and retention in rehabilitation research. *American Journal of Physical Medicine and Rehabilitation, 87,* 330–338.

Berger, L. K., Begun, A. L., & Otto-Salaj, L. L. (2009). Participant recruitment in intervention research: Scientific integrity and cost-effective strategies. *International Journal of Social Research Methodology, 12,* 79–92.

Berger, L., Brondino, M., Fisher, M., Gwyther, R., & Garbutt, J. C. (2016). Treatment of alcohol use disorder in a primary care setting: Pretreatment alcohol use and the role of drinking goal. *Journal of the American Board of Family Medicine, 29,* 37–49.

Berger, L., Fisher, M., Brondino, M., Bohn, M., Gwyther, R., Longo, L., . . . Garbutt, J. C. (2013). Efficacy of acamprosate for alcohol dependence in a family medicine setting in the United States: A randomized, double-blind, placebo-controlled study. *Alcoholism: Clinical and Experimental Research, 37,* 668–674.

Berry, D. M., & Bass, C. P. (2012). Successfully recruiting, surveying, and retaining college students: A description of methods for the risk, religiosity, and emerging adulthood study. *Research in Nursing and Health, 35,* 659–670.

Blaeser, L. M., Rose, S. J., Demant, J., Barnett, J. P., Wooters, N., King, T., & Otto-Salaj, L. L. (2008, June). *Changing urban treatment infrastructure: Responses in recruitment strategies for an HIV RCT for inner-city women with alcohol use disorders.* Presented at the 2008 Annual Meeting of the Research Society on Alcoholism, Washington, DC.

BootsMiller, B. J., Ribisl, K. M., Mowbray, C. T., Davidson, W. S., Walton, M. A., & Herman, S. E. (1998). Methods of ensuring high follow-up rates: Lessons from a longitudinal study of dual diagnosed participants. *Substance Use and Misuse, 33,* 2665–2685.

Bowie, C. R., & Harvey, P. D. (2006). Administration and interpretation of the Trail Making Test. *Nature Protocols, 1,* 2277–2281.

Boys, A., Marsden, J., Stillwell, G., Hatchings, K., Griffiths, P., & Farrell, M. (2003). Minimizing respondent attrition in longitudinal research: Practical implications from a study of adolescent drinking. *Journal of Adolescence, 26,* 363–373.

Brandt, A. M. (1978). Racism and research: The case of the Tuskegee Syphilis Study. *Hastings Center Magazine.* Retrieved from http://www.med.navy.mil/bumed/Documents/Healthcare%20Ethics/Racism-And-Research.pdf.

Braver, S., & Smith, M. (1996). Maximizing both external and internal validity in longitudinal true experiments with voluntary treatments: The "combined modified" design. *Evaluation and Program Planning, 19,* 2887–300. doi: 10.1016/S0149-7189(96)0009-8

Brekke, J. (2005). Commentary. In L. B. Alexander & P. Solomon (Eds), *The research process in the human services: Behind the scenes* (pp. 56–65). Belmont, CA: Thomson, Brooks/Cole.

Brocato, J., & Wagner, E. F. (2008). Predictors of retention in an alternative-to-prison substance abuse treatment program. *Criminal Justice and Behavior, 35,* 99–119. doi: 10.1177/0093854807309429

Brown, B. A., Long, H. L., Gould, H., Weitz, T., & Milliken, N. (2000, July–August). A conceptual model for the recruitment of diverse women into research studies. *Journal of Women's Health and Gender-Based Medicine, 9,* 625–632.

Broyles, L. M., Binswanger, I. A., Jenkins, J., Finnell, D. S., Faseru, B., Cavaiola, A., . . . Gordon, A. J. (2014). Confronting inadvertent stigma and pejorative language in addiction scholarship: A recognition and response. *Substance Abuse, 35,* 217–221.

Broyles, L. M., Rosenberger, E., Hanusa, B. H., Kraemer, K. L., & Gordon, A. J. (2012). Hospitalized patients' acceptability of nurse-delivered screening, brief intervention, and referral to treatment. *Alcoholism: Clinical and Experimental Research, 36,* 725–731. doi: 10.1111/j.1530-0277.2011.01651.x

Burke, B. L., Arkowitz, H., & Menchola, M. (2003). The efficacy of motivational interviewing: A meta-analysis of controlled clinical trials. *Journal of Consulting and Clinical Psychology, 71,* 843–861.

Castro, F. G., Harmon, M. P., Coe, K., & Tafoya-Barraza, H. M. (1994). Drug prevention research with Hispanic populations: Theoretical and methodological issues and a generic structural model. In A. Cázares & L. A. Beatty (Eds.), *Scientific methods for prevention intervention research* (pp. 203–234). Research Monograph No. 139. Rockville, MD: National Institute on Drug Abuse.

CenterWatch. (2013). *The process of informed consent.* Alexandria, VA: Association of Clinical Research Professionals (ACRP).

Cepeda, A., & Valdez, A. (2010). Ethnographic strategies in the tracking and retention of street-recruited community-based samples of substance using hidden populations in longitudinal studies. *Substance Use and Misuse, 45,* 700–716.

Charlson, M. E., & Horowitz, R. I. (1984). Applying results of randomized trials to clinical practice: Impact of losses before randomization. *British Medical Journal, 289,* 1281–1284.

Claus, R. E., Kindleberger, L. R., & Dugan, M. C. (2002). Predictors of attrition in a longitudinal study of substance abusers. *Journal of Psychoactive Drugs, 34,* 69–74.

Clay, C., Ellis, M. A., Amodeo, M., Fassler, I., & Griffin, M. L. (2003). Recruiting a community sample of African American subjects: The nuts and bolts of a successful effort. *Families in Society: The Journal of Contemporary Human Services, 84,* 396–404.

ClinicalTrials.gov. (2014). *ClinicalTrials.gov background.* Retrieved from https://www.clinicaltrials.gov/ct2/about-site/background

Clough, A., Wagman, J., Rollins, C., Barnes, J., Connor-Smith, J., Holditch-Niolon, P., . . . Glass, N. (2011). The SHARE Project: Maximizing participant retention in a longitudinal study with victims of intimate partner violence. *Field Methods, 23,* 86–101.

Cohen, J. (1988). *Statistical power analysis for the behavioral sciences* (2nd ed.). Hillsdale, NJ: Erlbaum.

Cohen, J. (1992). A power primer. *Psychological Bulletin, 112,* 155–159.

COMBINE Study Research Group, The. (2003). Testing combined pharmacotherapies and behavioral interventions for alcohol dependence (The COMBINE Study): A pilot feasibility study. *Alcoholism: Clinical and Experimental Research, 27,* 1123–1131.

Cotter, R. B., Burke, J. D., Loeber, R., & Navratil, J. L. (2002). Innovative retention methods in longitudinal research: A case study of the developmental trends study. *Journal of Child and Family Studies, 11,* 485–498.

Cotter, R. B., Burke, J. D., Stouthamer-Loeber, M., & Loeber, R. (2005). Contacting participants for follow-up: How much effort is required to retain participants in longitudinal studies? *Evaluation and Program Planning, 28,* 15–21.

Cottler, L., Compton, W., Ben-Abdallah, A., Horne, M., & Claverie, D. (1996). Achieving a 96.6% follow-up rate in a longitudinal study of drug abusers. *Drug and Alcohol Dependence, 41,* 209–217.

Couper, M. P., Alexander, G. L., Zhang, N., Little, R. J. A., Maddy, N., Nowak, M. A., . . . Johnson, C. C. (2010). Engagement and retention: Measuring breadth and depth of participant use of an online intervention. *Journal of Medical Internet Research, 12,* e52. doi: 10.2196/jmir.1430

Corcoran, J., & Secret, M. (2013). *Social work research skills workbook: A step-by-step guide to conducting agency-based research.* New York, NY: Oxford University Press.

Corrigan, O., & Tutton, R. (2006). What's in a name? Subjects, volunteers, participants and activists in clinical research. *Clinical Ethics, 1,* 101–104.

Craigslist About Factsheet. (n.d.). Retrieved from https://www.craigslist.org/about/factsheet

Creswell, J. W., & Plano Clark, V. L. (2011). *Designing and conducting mixed methods research* (2nd ed.). Thousand Oaks, CA: Sage.

Czajkowski, S., Powell, L., & Spring, B. (n.d.). *Models and methods in behavioral intervention development research* [PowerPoint Slides]. Retrieved from http://www.sbm.org/meeting/2011/presentations/tuesday/Susan%20Czajkowski.pdf

Danchak, C. (n.d.). *The pulse on recruitment.* Alexandria, VA: CenterWatch.

Dattalo, P. (2008). *Determining sample size: Balancing power, precision, and practicality.* Pocket Guides to Social Work Research. New York, NY: Oxford University Press.

Dattalo, P. (2010). *Strategies to approximate random sampling and assignment.* Pocket Guides to Social Work Research. New York, NY: Oxford University Press.

David, M. C., Alati, R., Ware, R. S., & Kinner, S. A. (2013). Attrition in a longitudinal study with hard-to-reach participants was reduced by ongoing contact. *Journal of Clinical Epidemiology, 76,* 575–581.

Davis, L., Broome, M., & Cox, R. (2002). Maximizing retention in community-based trials. *Journal of Nursing Scholarship, 34*(1), 47–53.

Delva, J., Allen-Meares, P., & Momper, S. L. (2010). *Cross-cultural research.* New York, NY: Oxford University Press.

Desmond, D. P., Maddux, J. F., Johnson, T. H., & Confer, B. A. (1995). Obtaining follow-up interviews for treatment evaluation. *Journal of Substance Abuse Treatment, 12,* 95–102.

Diaz-Ordaz, K., Kenward, M. G., Cohen, A., Coleman, C. L., & Eldridge, S. (2014). Are missing data adequately handled in cluster randomized trials? A systematic review and guidelines. *Clinical Trials, 11,* 590–600.

DiClemente, R., & Wingood, G. M. (1998). Monetary incentives: A useful strategy for enhancing enrollment and promoting participation in HIV/STD risk reduction interventions [Editorial: Comment]. *Sexually Transmitted Infections, 74,* 239–240.

Dillman, D. A. (1978). *Mail and telephone surveys: The total design method.* New York, NY: Wiley.

Eichenwald, K., & Kolata, G. (1999). Drug trials hide conflicts for doctors. *New York Times.* Retrieved from http://www.nytimes.com/1999/05/16/business/drug-trials-hide-conflicts-for-doctors.html?pagewanted=all

Engel, R. J., & Schutt, R. K. (2017). *The practice of research in social work* (4th ed.). Thousand Oaks, CA: Sage.

Epstein, E. E., Drapkin, M. L., Yusko, D. A., Cook, S. M., McCrady, B. S., & Jensen, N. K. (2005). Is alcohol assessment therapeutic? Pretreatment change in drinking among alcohol-dependent women. *Journal of Studies in Alcohol, 66,* 369–378.

Farabee, D., Hawken, A., Calhoun, S., Veliz, S., Veliz, R., Grossman, J., & Zhang, Y. (2016). Tracking and locating itinerant subjects with a rechargeable incentive card: Results of a randomized trial. *Substance Use and Misuse, 51,* 658–663.

Farabee, D., Hawken, A., & Griffith, P. (2011). Tracking and incentivizing substance abusers in longitudinal research: Results of a survey of NIDA-funded investigators. *Journal of Addiction Medicine, 5,* 878–91.

Farmer, A. Y., & Farmer, G. L. (2014). *Research with diverse groups: Research designs and multivariate latent modeling for equivalence.* Pocket Guides for Social Work Research. New York, NY: Oxford University Press.

Faulkner, S. S., & Faulkner, C. A. (2014). *Research methods for social workers: A practice-based approach* (2nd ed.). Chicago, IL: Lyceum.

Festinger, D. S., Dugosh, K. L., Croft, J. R., Arabia, P. L., & Marlowe, D. B. (2010). Corrected feedback: A procedure to enhance recall of informed consent to research among substance abusing offenders. *Ethics and Behavior, 20,* 387–399. doi: 10.1080/10508422.2010.491767

Festinger, D. S., Marlowe, D. B., Croft, J. R., Dugosh, K. L., Arabia, P. L., & Benasutti, K. M. (2009). Monetary incentives improve recall of research consent information: It pays to remember. *Experimental and Clinical Psychopharmacology, 17,* 99–104. doi: 10.1037/a0015421

Festinger, D. S., Marlowe, D. B., Croft, J. R., Dugosh, K. L., Mastro, N. K., Lee, P. A., . . . Patapis, N. S. (2005). Do research payments precipitate drug use or coerce participation? *Drug and Alcohol Dependence, 78,* 275–281.

Fisher, L. D., Dixon, D. O., Herson, J., Frankowski, R. K., Hearron, M. S., & Peace, K. E. (1990). Intention to treat in clinical trials. In K. E. Peace (Ed.), *Statistical issues in drug research and development* (pp. 331–350). New York, NY: Dekker.

Fraser, M. W., Richman, J. M., Galinsky, M. J., & Day, S. H. (2009). *Intervention research: Developing social programs.* New York, NY: Oxford University Press.

Freedman, B. (1987). Scientific value and validity as ethical requirements for research: A proposed explication. *IRB, 9,* 7–10.

Garner, B. R., Passetti, L. L., Orndorff, M. G., & Godley, S. H. (2007). Reasons for and attitudes toward follow-up research participation among adolescents enrolled in an outpatient substance abuse treatment program. *Journal of Child and Adolescent Substance Abuse, 16*(4), 45–57.

Gerstein, D. R., & Johnson, R. A. (2000). Nonresponse and selection bias in treatment follow-up studies. *Substance Use and Misuse, 35,* 971–1014.

Glaze, L. E., & Maruschak, L. M. (2008). *Parents in prison and their minor children.* Retrieved from http://www.bjs.gov/index.cfm?ty=pbdetail&iid=823

Gorringe, J. A. L. (1970). Initial preparation for clinical trials. In E. L. Harris & J. D. Fitzgerald (Eds.), *The principles and practice of clinical trials* (pp. 41–46). Edinburgh/London, UK: Livingstone.

Grady, D., Cummings, S. R., & Hulley, S. B. (2001). Designing an experiment: Clinical trials, II. In S. B. Hulley, S. R. Cummings, W. S. Browner, D. Grady, N. Hearst, & T. B. Newman (Eds.), *Designing clinical research* (2nd ed., pp. 157–174). Philadelphia, PA: Lippincott Williams & Wilkins.

Grant, S., Montgomery, P., Hopewell, S., Macdonald, G., Moher, D., & Mayo-Wilson, E. (2013). Developing a reporting guideline for social and psychological intervention trials. *Research on Social Work Practice, 23,* 595–602.

Greene, A. H. (2012). HIPAA compliance for clinician texting. *Journal of American Health Information Management Association, 83,* 34–36.

Greiner, K. A., Friedman, D. B., Adams, S. A., Gwede, C. K., Cupertino, P., Engelman, K. K., . . . Hébert, J. R. (2014). Effective recruitment strategies and community-based participatory research: Community networks program centers' recruitment in cancer prevention studies. *Cancer Epidemiology, Biomarkers and Prevention, 23,* 416–423. doi: 10.1158/1055-9965.EPI-13-0760

Grinnell, R. M., & Unrau, Y. A. (2014). *Social work research and evaluation: Foundations of evidence-based practice* (10th ed.). NewYork, NY: Oxford University Press.

Guo, S., Barth, R., & Gibbons, C. (2004). *Introduction to propensity score matching: A new device for program evaluation.* Workshop presented at the annual conference of the Society for Social Work Research (SSWR), New Orleans (January). Retrieved August 20, 2011, from http://ssw.unc.edu/VRC/Lectures/PSM_SSWR_2004.pdf

Halpern, S. D., Karlawish, J. H. T., & Berlin, J. A. (2002). The continuing unethical conduct of underpowered clinical trials. *Journal of the American Medical Association (JAMA), 288,* 358–362.

Hansen, W. B., Tobler, N. S., & Graham, J. W. (1990). Attrition in substance abuse prevention research: A meta-analysis of 85 longitudinally followed cohorts. *Evaluation Review, 14,* 677–685.

Hollis, S., & Campbell, F. (1999, September). What is meant by intention to treat analysis? Survey of published randomised controlled trials. *British Medical Journal, 319,* 670–674.

Israel, B. A., Schulz, A. J., Parker, E. A., & Becker, A. B. (1998). Review of community-based research: Assessing partnership approaches to improve public health. *Annual Review of Public Health, 19,* 173–202. doi: 10.1146/annurev.publhealth.19.1.173

Johnson, M. O., & Remien, R. H. (2003). Adherence to research protocols in a clinical context: Challenges and recommendations from behavioral intervention trials. *American Journal of Psychotherapy, 57,* 348–360.

Kamb, M. L., Rhodes, F., Hoxworth, T., Rogers, J., Lentz, A., Kent, C., . . . Peterman, T. A. (1998). What about money? Effect of small monetary incentives on enrollment, retention, and motivation to change behaviour in an HIV/STD prevention counseling intervention. The Project RESPECT Study Group. *Sexually Transmitted Infections, 74,* 253–255.

Kavanaugh, I., Moro, T. T., Savage, T., & Mehendale, R. (2006). Enacting a theory of caring to recruit and retain vulnerable participants for sensitive research. *Research in Nursing and Health, 29,* 244–252.

Keller, C., Gonzales, A., & Fleuriet, K. (2005). Retention of minority participants in clinical research studies. *Western Journal of Nursing Research, 27,* 292–306.

Kingston, D., McDonald, S., Biringer, A., Austin, M. P., Hegadoren, K., McDonald, S., . . . van Zanten, S. V. (2014). Comparing the feasibility, acceptability, clinical-, and cost-effectiveness of mental health e-screening to paper-based screening on the detection of depression, anxiety, and psychosocial risk in pregnant women: A study protocol of a randomized, parallel-group, superiority trial. *Trials, 15*(3). doi: 10.1186/1745-6215-15-3. Retrieved from https://trialsjournal.biomedcentral.com/articles/10.1186/1745-6215-15-3

Kitterman, D. R., Cheng, S. K., Dilts, D. M., & Orwoll, E. S. (2011). The prevalence and economic impact of low-enrolling clinical studies at an academic medical center. *Academic Medicine: Journal of Association of American Medical Colleges, 86,* 1360–1366.

Kleschinsky, J. H., Bosworth, L. B., Nelson, S. E., Walsh, E. K., & Shaffer, H. J. (2009). Persistence pays off: Follow-up methods for difficult-to-track longitudinal samples. *Journal of Studies on Alcohol and Drugs, 70,* 751–761.

Kraemer, H. C., Mintz, J., Noda, A., Tinklenberg, J., & Yesavage, J. A. (2006). Caution regarding the use of pilot studies to guide power calculations for study proposals. *Archives of General Psychiatry, 63,* 484–489.

Krysik, J. L., & Finn, J. (2013). *Research for effective social work practice* (3rd ed.). New York, NY: Routledge.

Lamberti, M. J., Mathias, A., Getz, K., Myles, J. E., & Howe, D. (2012). Evaluating the impact of patient recruitment and retention practices. *Drug Information Journal, 46,* 573–580.

Larsen, D. L., Attkisson, C. C., Hargreaves, W. A., & Nguyen, T. D. (1979). Assessment of client/patient satisfaction: Development of a general scale. *Evaluation and Program Planning, 2,* 197–207.

Lauby, J., Kotranski, L., Feighan, K., Collier, K., Semaan, S., & Halberg, J. (1996). Effects of intervention attrition and research attrition on the evaluation of an HIV prevention program. *Journal of Drug Issues, 26,* 663–677.

Lee, C. S., Hayes, R. B., McQuaid, E. L., & Borrelli, B. (2010). Predictors of retention in smoking cessation treatment among Latino smokers in the Northeast United States. *Health Education Research, 25,* 687–697.

Lee, M. Y., & Zaharlick, A. (2013). *Culturally competent research: Using ethnography as a meta-framework.* Pocket Guides to Social Work Research Methods. New York, NY: Oxford University Press.

Leonard, N. R., Lester, P., Rotheram-Borus, M. J., Mattes, K., Gwadz, M., & Ferns, B. (2003). Successful recruitment and retention of participants in longitudinal behavioral research. *AIDS Education and Prevention, 15,* 269–281.

Lidz, C. W., Appelbaum, P. S., & Meisel, A. (1988). Two models of implementing informed consent. *Archives of Internal Medicine, 148,* 1385–1389. doi: 10.1001/archinte.1988.00380060149027

Little, R., & Kang, S. (2015). Intention-to-treat analysis with treatment discontinuation and missing data in clinical trials. *Statistics in Medicine, 34,* 2381–2390.

Mahoney, S. (2009, May 26). *Common rating scales to use when writing questions* [Web log comment]. Retrieved from http://blog.verint.com/common-rating-scales-to-use-when-writing-questions

Mann, K., Lehert, P., & Morgan, M. Y. (2004). Abstinence in alcohol-dependent individuals: Results of a meta-analysis. *Alcoholism: Clinical and Experimental Research, 28*(1), 51–63.

Mantry, D., Cooper, S.-A., Smiley, E., Morrison, J., Allan, L., Williamson, A., . . . Jackson, A. (2008). The prevalence and incidence of mental ill-health in adults with Down syndrome. *Journal of Intellectual Disability Research, 52,* 141–155. doi: 10.1111/j.1365-2788.2007.00985.x

Marchant-Shapiro, T. (2013). The luck of the Irish: Sampling green M&M's. In B. P. Skott & M. Ward (Eds.), *Active learning exercises for research methods in social sciences* (pp. 8–10). Thousand Oaks, CA: Sage.

Materia, F. T., Miller, E. A., Runion, M. C., Chesnut, R. P., Irvin, J. B., Richardson, C. B., & Perkins, D. F. (2016). Let's get technical: Enhancing program evaluation through the use and integration of Internet and mobile technologies. *Evaluation and Program Planning, 56,* 31–42.

McGregor, L., Parker, K., LeBlanc, P., & King, K. M. (2010). Using social exchange theory to guide successful study recruitment and retention: Social exchange theory can be used to reduce participant attrition during studies, as Lisa McGregor, Karen Parker, Pamela LeBlanc and Kathryn M. King explain. *Nurse Researcher, 17*(2), 74–82.

McKay, M. M. (2005). Commentary. In L. B. Alexander & P. Solomon (Eds.), *The research process in the human services: Behind the scenes* (pp. 14–19). Belmont, CA: Thomson, Brooks/Cole.

McMahon, R. C., Kelley, A., & Kouzekanani, K. (1993). Personality and coping styles in the prediction of dropout from treatment for cocaine abuse. *Journal of Personality Assessment, 61*, 147–155.

McMurtry, S. L., & Hudson, W. W. (2000). The Client Satisfaction Inventory: Results of an initial validation study. *Research on Social Work Practice, 10*, 644–663.

McMurtry, S. L., & Torres, J. B. (2002). Initial validation of a Spanish-language version of the Client Satisfaction Inventory. *Research on Social Work Practice, 12*, 124–142.

Meyers, K., Webb, A., Frantz, J., & Randall, M. (2003). What does it take to retrain substance-abusing adolescents in research protocols? Delineation of effort required, strategies undertaken, cost incurred, and 6-month post-treatment differences by retention difficulty. *Drug and Alcohol Dependence, 69*(1), 73–85.

Miller, W. R., & Manuel, J. K. (2008). How large must a treatment effect be before it matters to practitioners? An estimation method and demonstration. *Drug and Alcohol Review, 27*, 524–528.

Molenberghs, G., Fitzmaurice, G., Kenward, M. G., Tsiatis, A., & Verbeke, G. (2015). *Handbook of missing data methodology*. Boca Raton, FL: CRC Press/Taylor & Francis.

Moodley, K., Pather, M., & Myer, L. (Eds.). (2005). Informed consent and participant perceptions of influenza vaccine trials in South Africa. *Journal of Medical Ethics, 31*, 727–732. doi: 10.1136/jme.2004.009910

Morgan, A. J., Jorm, A. F., & Mackinnon, A. J. (2013). Internet-based recruitment to a depression prevention intervention: Lessons from the mood memos study. *Journal of Medical Internet Research, 15*(2). doi: 10.2196/jmir.2262. Retrieved from http://www.jmir.org/2013/2/e31/

Moser, D. K., Dracup, K., & Doering, L. V. (2000). Factors differentiating dropouts from completers in a longitudinal multicenter clinical trial. *Nursing Research, 49*, 109–116.

Mueser, K. T., Glynn, S. M., Cather, C., Zarate, R., Fox, L., Feldman, J., ... Clark, R. E. (2009). Family intervention for co-occurring substance use and severe psychiatric disorders: Participant characteristics and correlates of initial engagement and more extended exposure in a randomized controlled trial. *Addictive Behaviors, 34*, 867–877.

Murphy, F. G., Jackson, P. A., Johnson, P. S., Ofili, E., Quarshie, A., & Nwigwe, C. (2004). Informing and consenting disadvantaged populations for clinical and community-based research studies. *American Journal of Health Studies, 19*, 246–253.

National Institutes of Health (NIH). (2012). *Grants and funding: Glossary*. Retrieved from http://grants.nih.gov/grants/policy/hs/glossary.htm

Navratil, J. L., Green, S. M., Loeber, R., & Lahey, B. B. (1994). Minimizing subject loss in a longitudinal study of deviant behavior. *Journal of Child and Family Studies, 3,* 89–106.

Nemes, S., Wish, E., Wraight, B., & Messina, N. (2002). Correlates of treatment follow-up difficulty. *Substance Use and Misuse, 37*(1), 19–45.

Nguyen, T. D., Attkisson, C. C., & Stegner, B. L. (1984). Assessment of patient satisfaction: Development and refinement of a service evaluation questionnaire. *Evaluation and Program Planning, 6,* 299–314.

O'Connell, B., O'Shea, D., & Gallagher, S. (2014). Feasibility study investigating the use of Amazon's Mechanical Turk for online positive psychology intervention trials. *Bulletin of the European Health Psychology Society, 16* (supplement). Retrieved from http://www.ehps.net/ehp/index.php/contents/article/view/658/651

Palmer, V. J., Yelland, J. S., & Taft, A. J. (2011). Ethical complexities of screening for depression and intimate partner violence (IPV) in intervention studies. *BMC Public Health, 11*(Suppl. 5). doi: 10.1186/1471-2458-11-S5-S3

Pappas, D. M., Werch, C. E., & Carlson, J. M. (1998). Recruitment and retention in an alcohol prevention program at two inner-city middle schools. *Journal of School Health, 68,* 231–236.

Passetti, L. L., Godley, S. H., Scott, C. K., & Siekmann, M. (2000). A low-cost follow-up resource: Using the World Wide Web to maximize client location efforts. *American Journal of Evaluation, 21,* 195–203.

Patton, R., Slesnick, N., Bantchevska, D., Guo, X., & Kim, Y. (2011). Predictors of follow-up completion among runaway substance-abusing adolescents and their primary caretakers. *Community Mental Health Journal, 47,* 220–226. doi: 10.1007/s10597-009-9281-9

Perez, S. (2010). Twitter is NOT a social network, says twitter exec. *readwrite.* Retrieved from http://readwrite.com/2010/09/14/twitter_is_not_a_social_network_says_twitter_exec/

Pettus-Davis, C., Howard, M. O., Murugan, V., Roberts-Lewis, A., Scheyett, A. M., Botnick, C., & Vance, M. (2015). Acceptability of a social support intervention for re-entering prisoners. *Journal of the Society for Social Work and Research, 6,* 51–89.

Post, E. P., Cruz, M., & Harman, J. (2006). Incentive payments for attendance at appointments for depression among low-income African-Americans. *Psychiatric Services, 57,* 414–416. http://dx.doi.org/10.1176/appi.ps.57.3.414

Prinz, R. J., Smith, E. P., Dumas, J. E., Laughlin, J. E., White, D. W., & Barron, R. (2001). Recruitment and retention of participants in prevention trials involving family-based interventions. *American Journal of Preventive Medicine, 20,* 31–37.

Reitan, R. M. (1959). *Trail Making Test: Manual for the administration and scoring of the Trail Making Test.* Bloomington: Indiana University Press.

Resko, S., Agius, E., Hudek, B., Brown, S., Kondrat, D. C., & Kral, M. (2017). *Recruiting young adults through Facebook advertisements.* Presented at the annual meetings of the Society for Social Work and Research (SSWR), New Orleans (January). (Images shared with permission.)

Ribisl, K., Waltron, M., Mowbray, C., Luke, D., Davidson II, W., & BootsMiller, B. (1996). Minimizing participant attrition in panel studies through the use of effective retention and tracking strategies: Review and recommendations. *Evaluation and Program Planning, 19,* 1–25.

Richy, F. F., & Mawet, A. M. (2007). Evidence-biased medicine: Intention-to-treat analysis less conservative? *Internet Journal of Epidemiology, 4*(1), 1.

Rifkin, A. (2013). Tumblr is not what you think. *TechCrunch.* Retrieved from http://techcrunch.com/2013/02/18/tumblr-is-not-what-you-think/

Robinson, K. A., Dennison, C. R., Wayman, D. M., Pronovost, P. J., & Needham, D. M. (2007). Systematic review identifies number of strategies important for retaining study participants. *Journal of Clinical Epidemiology, 60,* 757–765.

Roffman, R. A., Klepsch, R., Wertz, J. S., Simpson, E. E., & Stephens, R. S. (1993). Predictors of attrition from an outpatient marijuana-dependence counseling program. *Addictive Behaviors, 18,* 553–566.

Rosenthal, J. A. (2012). *Statistics and data interpretation for social work.* New York, NY: Springer.

Rouse, M. (2015). LinkedIn. *WhatIs.com.* Retrieved from http://whatis.techtarget.com/definition/LinkedIn

Royse, D. (2011). *Research methods in social work* (6th ed.). Belmont, CA: Brooks/Cole Cengage Learning.

Rubin, A. (2009). *Oxford bibliographies: Social work research methods.* Retrieved from www.oxfordbibliogaphies.com/view/document/obo-9780195389678/obo-978195389678-0008.xml. doi: 10.1093/OBO/9780195389678-0008

Rubin, A., & Babbie, E. R. (2014). *Research methods for social work* (8th ed.). Belmont, CA: Brooks/Cole CENGAGE Learning.

Rubin, A., & Babbie, E. (2016). *Essential research methods for social work* (4th ed.). Boston, MA: Cengage Learning.

Rumpf, H. J., Bischof, G., Hapke, U., Meyer, C., & John, U. (2000). Studies on natural recovery from alcohol dependence: Sample selection bias by media solicitation? *Addiction, 95,* 765–775. doi: 10.1046/j.1360-0443.2000.95576512.x

Russell, A. C. (2014). *A hands-on manual for social work research.* Chicago, IL: Lyceum.

Saitz, R., Palfai, T. P., Cheng, D. M., Horton, N. J., Dukes, K., Kraemer, K. L., Roberts, M., . . . Samet, J. H. (2009). Some medical inpatients with unhealthy alcohol use may benefit from brief intervention. *Journal of Studies on Alcohol and Drugs, 70,* 426–435.

Sage, G. P. (1994). Drug prevention research with Native-American populations: Some considerations. In A. Cázares & L. A. Beatty (Eds.), *Scientific methods for prevention intervention research* (pp. 235–248). Research Monograph No. 139. Rockville, MD: National Institute on Drug Abuse.

Schechter, D., & Lebovitch, R. (2005). Normal controls are expensive to find: Methods to improve cost-effectiveness of the screening evaluation. *Psychiatry Research, 136,* 69–78. doi: 10.1016/j.psychres.2005.06.002

Schwartz, J. A., & Beaver, K. M. (2014). A biosocial analysis of the sources of missing data in criminological research. *Journal of Criminal Justice, 42,* 452–461.

Scott, C. K. (2004). A replicable model for achieving over 90% follow-up rates in longitudinal studies of substance abusers. *Drug and Alcohol Dependence, 74,* 21–36.

Seddon, T. (2005). Paying drug users to take part in research: Justice, human rights and business perspectives on the use of incentive payments. *Addiction Research and Theory, 13,* 101–109. doi: 10.1080/16066350512331328122

Shao, W., Guan, W., Clark, M. A., Liu, T., Santelices, C. C., Cortes, D. E., & Merchant, R. C. (2015). Variations in recruitment yield, costs, speed and participant diversity across Internet platforms in a global study examining the efficacy of an HIV/AIDS and HIV testing animated and live-action video among English- or Spanish-speaking Internet or social media users. *Digital Culture and Education, 7*(1), 40–86.

Shavers, V. L., Lynch, C. F., & Burmeister, L. F. (2002). Racial differences in factors that influence the willingness to participate in medical research studies. *Annals of Epidemiology, 12,* 248–256. doi: 10.1016/S1047-2797(01)00265-4

Shere, M., Zhao, X. Y., & Koren, G. (2014). The role of social media in recruiting for clinical trials in pregnancy. *PLoS ONE, 9,* e92744. doi: 10.1371/journal.pone.0092744

Sink, C. A., & Mvududu, N. H. (2010). Statistical power, sampling, and effect sizes: Three keys to research relevancy. *Counseling Outcome Research and Evaluation, 1,* 1–18.

Skloot, R. (2010). *The immortal life of Henrietta Lacks.* New York, NY: Broadway Paperbacks/Random House.

Slavin, R., & Smith, D. (2009). The relationship between sample sizes and effect sizes in systematic reviews in education. *Educational Evaluation and Policy Analysis, 31,* 500–506.

Smith, J. E., & Meyers, R. J. (2004). *Motivating substance abusers to enter treatment: Working with family members.* The CRAFT Intervention Program. New York, NY: Guilford Press.

Snowden, L. R. (2005). Commentary. In L. B. Alexander & P. Solomon (Eds.), *The research process in the human services: Behind the scenes* (pp. 472–480). Belmont, CA: Thomson, Brooks/Cole.

Sobell, L. C., Maisto, S. A., Sobell, M. B., & Cooper, A. M. (1979). Reliability of alcohol abusers' self-reports of drinking behavior. *Behaviour Research and Therapy, 17,* 157–160. doi: 10.1016/0005-7967(79)90025-1

Solomon, P., Cavanaugh, M. M., & Draine, J. (2009). Randomized controlled trials: Design and implementation for community-based psychosocial interventions. New York, NY: Oxford University Press.

Spilker, B., & Cramer, J. A. (1992). *Patient recruitment in clinical trials.* New York, NY: Raven Press.

Sramek, J., Hauptmann, K., Ding, H., Fern, K., Cutler, N. R., & Adcock, S. (2015). *Survey of healthy participants in Phase 1 trials. Applied Clinical Trials.* Retrieved from http://www.appliedclinicaltrialsonline.com/survey-healthy-participants-phase-i-trials

Stanford, P. D., Monte, D. A., Briggs, F. M., Flynn, P. M., Tanney, M., Ellenberg, J. H., . . . Rogers, A. S. (2003). Recruitment and retention of adolescent participants in HIV research: Findings from the REACH (Reaching for Excellence in Adolescent Care and Health) project. *Journal of Adolescent Health, 32,* 192–203.

Stasiewicz, P., & Stalker, R. (1999). A comparison of three interventions on pretreatment dropout rates in an outpatient substance abuse clinic. *Addictive Behaviors, 24,* 579–582.

Sterling, R. L. (2011). Genetic research among the Havasuapi—A cautionary tale. *AMA Journal of Ethics, 13,* 113–117. Retrieved from http://journalofethics.ama-assn.org/2011/02/hlaw1-1102.html

Sterne, J. A. C., White, I. R., Carlin, J. B., Spratt, M., Royston, P., Kenward, M. G., Wood, A. M., & Carpenter, J. R. (2009, June 29). Multiple imputation for missing data in epidemiological and clinical research: Potential and pitfalls. *BMJ, 338.* Retrieved from http://www.bmj.com/content/338/bmj.b2393

Subbaraman, M. S., Laudet, A. B., Ritter, L. A., Stunz, A., & Kaskutas, L. A. (2015). Multisource recruitment strategies for advancing addiction recovery research beyond treated samples. *Journal of Community Psychology, 43,* 560–575. doi: 10.1002/jcop.21702

Sullivan, G. M., & Feinn, R. (2012). Using effect size—or why the *p* value is not enough. *Journal of Graduate Medical Education, 4,* 279–282.

Taylor, S. A. (2009). Engaging and retaining vulnerable youth in a short-term longitudinal qualitative study. *Qualitative Social Work, 8,* 391–408.

Thoma, A., Farrokhyar, F., McKnight, L., & Bhandari, M. (2010). Practical tips for surgical research: How to optimize patient recruitment. *Canadian Journal of Surgery, 53,* 205–210.

Thomson CenterWatch. (2006). *State of the clinical trials industry: A sourcebook of charts and statistics*. Boston, MA: Author.

Tiffany, J. S. (2006). Respondent-driven sampling in participatory research contexts: Participant-driven recruitment. *Journal of Urban Health, 83,* 113–124.

Toerien, M., Brookes, S. T., Metcalfe, C., de Salis, I., Tomlin, Z., Peters, T. J., . . . Donovan, J. L. (2009). A review of reporting of participant recruitment and retention in RCTs in six major journals. *Trials, 10,* 52. doi: 10.1186/1745-6215-10-52

Tran, T., Nguyen, T., & Chan, K. (2017). *Developing cross-cultural measurement in social work research and evaluation*. Pocket Guides to Social Work Research. New York, NY: Oxford University Press.

Trochim, W. M., Donnelly, J. P., & Arora, K. (2016). *Research methods: The essential knowledge base*. Boston, MA: Cengage Learning.

University of Pennsylvania Institutional Review Board (IRB). (2015). *Guidance on recruitment and research using social media*. Retrieved from http://www.upenn.edu/IRB/sites/default/files/IRB%20Social%20Media%20Guidance_March%202015_FINAL%20%282%29.pdf

University of Pittsburgh Institutional Review Board (IRB). (2014). *IRB guidance: Finder's fees and payments to research and clinical staff*. Retrieved from http://www.irb.pitt.edu/sites/default/files/Guidance/forms/FinderFees_4.1.2014.pdf

US Department of Health and Human Services. (1978). *The Belmont Report: Ethical principles and guidelines for the protection of human subjects of research*. Washington, DC. The National Commission for the Protection of Human Subjects of Biomedical and Behavioral Research. Retrieved from https://www.hhs.gov/ohrp/regulations-and-policy/belmont-report

Vander Stoep, A. (1999). Maintaining high subject retention in follow-up studies of children with mental illness. *Journal of Child and Family Studies, 8,* 305–318.

VanderWalde, A., & Kurzban, S. (2011). Paying human subjects in research: Where are we, how did we get here, and now what? *Public Health Reform, 39,* 543–558.

van der Wouden, J. C., Blankenstein, A. H., Huibers, M. J., van der Windt, D. A., Stalman, W. A., & Verhagen, A. P. (2007). Survey among 78 studies showed that Lasagna's law holds in Dutch primary care research. *Journal of Clinical Epidemiology, 60,* 819–824. doi: 10.1016/j.jclinepi.2006.11.010

Verheggen, F. W., Nieman, F. H., Reerink, E., & Kok, G. J. (1998). Patient satisfaction with clinical trial participation. *International Journal for Quality in Health Care, 10,* 319–330.

Voyer, P., Lauzon, S., Collin, J., & O'Brien, S. (2008). Research method issue: Recruiting and retaining subjects in a research study. *Nurse Researcher, 15,* 12–25.

Wahab, S. (2005). Motivational interviewing and social work practice. *Journal of Social Work, 5,* 45–60.

Walton, M. A., Ramanathan, C. S., & Reischl, T. M. (1998). Tracking substance abusers in longitudinal research: Understanding follow-up tracking difficulty. *American Journal of Community Psychology, 26,* 233–253.

Wang, E. A., Aminawung, J. A., Wildeman, C., Ross, J. S., & Krumholz, H. M. (2014). High incarceration rates among black men enrolled in clinical studies may compromise ability to identify disparities. *Health Affairs, 33,* 848–855.

Webb, M. S., Seigers, D., & Wood, E. A. (2009). Recruiting African American smokers into intervention research: Relationships between recruitment strategies and participant characteristics. *Research in Nursing and Health, 32,* 86–95.

Wilcox, S., Shumaker, S. A., Bowen, D. J., Naughton, M. J., Rosal, M. C., Ludlam, S. E., . . . Stevens, S. (2001). Promoting adherence and retention to clinical trials in special populations: A women's health initiative workshop. *Controlled Clinical Trials, 22,* 279–289.

Williams, P. L., Van Dyke, R., Eagle, M. Smith, D., & Vincent, C. A. (2008). Association of site-specific and participant-specific factors with retention of children in a long-term pediatric HIV cohort study. *American Journal of Epidemiology, 167,* 1375–1386.

Winslow, E. B., Bonds, D., Wolchik, S., Sandler, I., & Braver, S. (2009). Predictors of enrollment and retention in a preventive parenting intervention for divorced families. *Journal of Primary Prevention, 30,* 151–172.

Wipke-Tevis, D. D., & Pickett, M. A. (2008). The impact of the Health Insurance Portability and Accountability Act on participant recruitment and retention. *Western Journal of Nursing Research, 30,* 39–53. doi: 10.1177/0193945907302666

Yetarian, J. D., Dowa, S. J., & Kelly, J. F. (2012). Ensuring retention in longitudinal studies: A practical evaluation of an intensive follow-up protocol and suggested adaptations. *International Journal of Social Research Methodology, 15,* 369–383.

Yuan, P., Bare, M. G., Johnson, M. O., & Saberi, P. (2014). Using online social media for recruitment of human immunodeficiency virus-positive participants: A cross-sectional survey. *Journal of Medical Internet Research, 16,* e117.

Zanis, D. A. (2005). Commentary. In L. B. Alexander & P. Solomon (Eds.), *The research process in the human services: Behind the scenes* (pp. 32–40). Belmont, CA: Thomson, Brooks/Cole.

Zayas, L. H., Cabassa, L. J., & Perez, M. C. (2005). Capacity-to-consent in psychiatric research: Development and preliminary testing of a screening tool. *Research on Social Work Practice, 15,* 545–556. doi: 10.1177/1049731505275867

Zweben, A., Barrett, D., Berger, L, & Murray, K. T. (2005). Recruiting and retaining participants in a combined behavioral and pharmacological clinical trial. *Journal of Studies on Alcohol, 66*(Suppl. 15), 72–81. doi: http://dx.doi.org/10.15288/jsas.2005.s15.72

Zweben, A., Donovan, D. M., Randall, C. L., Barrett, D., Dermen, K., Kabela, E., . . . Rosengren, D. (1994). Issues in the development of subject recruitment strategies and eligibility criteria in multi-site trials of matching. *Journal of Studies on Alcohol, 55*(Suppl. 12), 62–69.

Index

Tables, figures, and boxes are indicated by an italic *t*, *f*, and *b* following the page number.